iety
_____

The Perils of Adolescence

Marcel Lebrun

D1016768

ROWMAN & LITTLEFIELD EDUCATION

A division of

ROWMAN & LITTLEFIELD PUBLISHERS, INC.

Lanham • New York • Toronto • Plymouth, UK

Published by Rowman & Littlefield Education
A division of Rowman & Littlefield Publishers, Inc.
A wholly owned subsidary of The Rowman & Littlefield Publishing Group, Inc.
4501 Forbes Boulevard, Suite 200, Lanham, Maryland 20706
http://www.rowmaneducation.com

Estover Road, Plymouth PL6 7PY, United Kingdom

British Library Cataloguing in Publication Information Available

Library of Congress Cataloging-in-Publication Data

Lebrun, Marcel, 1957-
    Rebels in society : the perils of adolescence / Marcel Lebrun.
       p. cm.
    Includes bibliographical references.
    ISBN 978-1-61048-463-3 (cloth : alk. paper) — ISBN 978-1-61048-464-0
(pbk. : alk. paper) — ISBN 978-1-61048-465-7 (electronic)
    1. Problem youth—United States. 2. Juvenile delinquency—United States—
Prevention. 3. Juvenile delinquency. I. Title.
HV1431.L43 2012
364.360973—dc23   2011027904

Printed in the United States of America

Contents

Foreword

Rebels in Society: The Perils of Adolescence

Kim Williams, PhD

Nothing is more important than keeping children safe and healthy and nurturing their growing and developing brains and bodies. Sadly, in some cases, children develop psychopathologies that interrupt the more normal growth and development. These children not only put themselves at risk for harm, but also place others at risk as well with violent and troubling behaviors.

In Marcel Lebrun's new book he captures these topics that are rarely discussed or addressed when dealing with children and safety and violence. As a society we have struggled to figure out what to do with juvenile offenders who are sociopaths or serial killers or sexual offenders. Other topics, however, rarely discussed are child prostitution and child trafficking and the systems in which these children are placed and must function.

Lebrun brings all of these difficult topics out into the light, so that we may better understand them and do something to prevent and improve the lives of young people most at risk and harmed. In my own work with juvenile offenders, I know that too often these children are placed aside in alternative schools or facilities with limited resources and few opportunities for rehabilitation. In Lebrun's book, he addresses these issues and offers recommendations for improvement.

As a society we cannot continue to fail these young people. They need competent adults advocating on their behalf. Lebrun is starting the charge of advocacy here.

Preface

Looking at the underbelly of our society is often a tragic journey full of despair and hopelessness. Investigating and researching what happens to juveniles who become throwaways of our society or are caught in the juvenile justice system can be discouraging due to the lack of hope and success stories.

Juveniles seem to be the most vulnerable members of our society. They are caught in between the powerlessness of childhood and the autonomy of being an adult. They are at the mercy of the whims of the adults in their lives. It is not surprising that so many become rebels against the school, as well as parental and community systems.

How would you like it if everything you did was controlled by adults? Dysfunctional adults seem to comprise an overwhelming majority of the adults in juveniles that act out. The research and life experiences have shown over and over that juveniles that are supported by parents, school and community very rarely act out or run away and become part of the youths living on the streets. The majority of these youths are trying to escape a home or community that is destroying them as individuals or as a way of surviving. Any place is better than the one that they live in.

Youths as we know them are creatures of impulsivity and reaction. Very rarely do they think through any of their actions. They do not plan, they just do. This mode of operations obviously results in many situations that are life threatening or life ending. A youth who runs away with thirty dollars in his pocket to New York City is not going to be able to last very long on the streets. He will turn to prostitution, stealing, drug dealing, or gangs as a way to survive.

A young female who runs away puts herself at risk for rape, prostitution, the sex trade, drug abuse, homelessness, and possibly death at the hands of a bad trick or serial killer. Either way whether you are male or female the results are the same: the streets swallow you up and you become a statistic. Unfortunately so many runaway youths become victims of the ugliness of what exists on the streets of America. Very few of these youths make it into adulthood or what would be considered a normal all-American existence. They are often dead before they turn thirty.

Many youths who enter the streets or a life of dysfunctional behaviors and criminal behaviors become the responsibility of the community social service system or the criminal justice system. It is common knowledge that both systems are ill prepared to meet the demands of the sheer numbers of youths who are runaways, foster kids, and arrested for committing petty and serious crimes. The lack of funding and resources has been an issue for years.

The social service department is charged with looking after the safety and basic needs of these youths. The lack of adequate personnel to do follow ups and monitoring often results in youth disappearing and never found till they show up in another city, in jail or dead. The people in power of this system are not fully aware of how many youths they actually lose. There are just too many youths for the amount of resources. It is sad but the reality.

The criminal justice system is also overburdened with youths finding themselves caught in this net. The facilities and programs are inadequate to meet the needs of the volume of youths in detention centers, but also are inadequate to meet the challenges of youths with mental health issues, special needs, pathological tendencies, and severe acting-out behaviors.

The chapters on the prison and detention centers will give you a clear perspective on the reality of what it means to be caught in those systems. I have deliberately painted a picture that will give you a straight and unbiased look at the realities and the failings of this system.

America is one of the wealthiest countries in the world yet we have millions of youth who are compromised, abused, and on the streets. We as a society are not able to help this vulnerable population. We try, yet we continue to fail year after year. We invest money and resources but at the first sign of economic recession we slash programs. We are almost resigned to the fact that there has to be causalities in a society like America.

A whole generation of youth who are battling family abuse, poverty, unsafe communities, drug addiction, mental health issues, bullying, and an unsuccessful educational system are becoming prominent and growing in numbers. The statistics cited in chapter 1 will depress you as there are so many youths in crisis. The movement toward this underbelly continues daily.

The pipeline of youths in transition or on the run continues 24/7. There does not seem to be any slowing down of this phenomenon.

As you begin to read this book your mandate will be for you to recognize in your own home, school, and community where the youths that you know are at risk and hopefully intervene before it is too late for that particular youth. If a youth needs mental health support, find him or her the network of mental health professionals that will be able to intervene and get the youth the services they need. If a youth is engaging in criminal activity, give them skills to empower them to make better choices and so on.

As an adult who has received the necessary support, education, and training it is time to make use of those skills to empower the youth you may know or come into contact with daily because of the work you do. My request to you is after reading this book become involved; it starts with one person at a time. JUST DO IT.

A kid's life may depend on what you choose to do or not do. Doesn't every youth in America deserve the chance and have the right to a great life? It can be as simple as being aware of what is going on for this kid and intervening. The other piece is not to give up when the going gets really hard. It is so easy to walk away. It is much more difficult to stay involved.

It has been my experience that when you help another human being there is a sense of worth that develops within you. We as adults have a mandate to be involved. We are the protectors of our children and youth. We need to have the beliefs that all children and youth are worth saving no matter what their actions or behaviors are. Every life is worth something.

We cannot afford to lose a single child or youth to the streets. If we do lose them to those ugly and dangerous streets we need to figure out how to get them away and into a life that they value and want to live. Our challenge is to make sure we listen to what these youths want but also keep in mind what are the skills these kids need to be successful. The success or failure of getting these kids off the street will depend on what we offer them. The bait must be valued and attractive. We need to build trust with kids who have been disappointed over and over by adults.

Our system of care must be improved so that all youth get the services and supports they need to navigate the troubled waters of adolescence. It is my hope that this book will enable you to become more aware of all the issues that these youth face but also will challenge you to start thinking outside the box on how to help the youths that surround you every day.

Are you up for the challenge? Can you make a difference? Are you going to be the one adult who makes an impact and saves a life? Begin your journey of discovery and may you be successful with as many youths as you can. You may be their only hope.

1

Wake-up Call! Statistics Tell the Truth!

Youth living in the twenty-first century face many critical issues. These issues are not new and have remained fairly consistent in their presence throughout the decades. It seems ironic that we have become more technologically savvy and efficient in our everyday lives, yet we still have many children who are casualties of this new technological age.

We still have many poor, undernourished, neglected, abused, and violent teenagers and children who succeed in achieving an early death or incarceration. A sad fact is that many states are able to predict with a good level of accuracy how many prison beds they will need ten years down the road, based on school standardized tests and number of students at-risk or receiving specialized services in elementary school.

There are approximately 74 million children in the United States of America. "A child is born into poverty every 33 seconds. A child is abused or neglected every 35 seconds. A child is born uninsured every 39 seconds. A child dies before his or her first birthday every 18 minutes. A child or teen is killed by gunfire every 3 hours" (Children's Defense Fund 2009). Why the chaos? Why are the youth of America in such crisis?

Statistics are wake-up calls for politicians and a society as a whole. The following were reported by the Children's Defense Fund (2009). Almost 1 in 13 children in the United States, or 5.8 million, live in extreme poverty. In 2008, a family of four was classified as extremely poor if their household income was below $10,600, or half of the official poverty line. Young children are more likely than school-age children to live in extreme poverty.

The Children's Defense Fund states that "more than half of all poor children in the United States live in eight states: California, Texas, New York,

Florida, Illinois, Ohio, Georgia and Michigan. The child poverty rate was 18.2 percent as of January 2010."

There are more poor white, non-Hispanic children than black children. However,

Hispanic and black children are about three times more likely to live in poverty than white or non-Hispanic children. Children who live in inner cities, rural areas, the South, or in female-headed families are more likely to be poor (Children's Defense Fund 2009).

Children under age six are more likely to be poor than school-age children. Poverty and race are the primary factors underpinning the pipeline to prison. In fact, black juveniles are about four times as likely as their white peers to end up being incarcerated.

The number of poor children was at its lowest in 1973. Since 2000, both the number and the rate have risen. There are now 13.3 million poor children in the United States, an increase of 500,000 between 2008 and 2009. These numbers are expected to increase as families face the full impact of the recession.

The child poverty rate dropped substantially in the 1960s, then rose significantly in the early 1980s. Great strides were made in decreasing child poverty in the late 1990s, owing in part to the strong economy. However, the child poverty rate was higher in 2009 than at the beginning of the decade. Child poverty is closely tied to the overall health of the economy, rising in periods of recession.

More than 14 million children in America are poor, but they live in working families. Research in education has proven that children who live in poverty are more likely to lag behind their peers, are less healthy, trail in emotional and intellectual development and are less likely to graduate from high school. The extreme sad statistic is that the cycle will remain unbroken and they will become parents saddled with poverty. Keeping children in poverty costs a half trillion dollars in lost productivity, poorer health, and increased crime. To end child poverty there has to be investment in quality education, livable wages for families, child care support, and health coverage.

Poverty often comes with violence. There are many unintentional firearm injuries occurring throughout the United States. Unintentional shootings account for nearly 20 percent of all firearm related fatalities among children ages fourteen and under, compared with 3 percent for the entire U.S. population. The unintentional firearm injury death rate among children ages fourteen and under in the United States is nine time higher than in twenty-five other industrialized countries combined.

There are actions that can be taken to protect children from gun violence. We as a nation can begin to support common sense gun safety measures.

There has to be a more stringent enforcement of gun laws at the state and federal levels. Americans have to cease their fascination with guns. Firearms must be removed from homes where children are present: "Guns don't kill; people do." And we need to stress nonviolent values and conflict resolution. Children have to see that solving problems occurs through communication, not the use of force and bullets.

Our media are bombarded with images of guns, violence, and aggression. Many advocates of gun control also embark on campaigns to refuse to buy or use products that glamorize violence. How many video games are out there where your success as a player depends on how many people you can kill? Do we intentionally give children the subconscious message that you are a winner if you destroy all your adversaries?

Children and teens need alternative models to base their values upon. We as a society need to provide safe zones, both inside the house and outside in the community. Are we capable of changing a whole culture that is based in violence? If we look elsewhere in the world, violence to this degree is not present.

"Approximately one-third of families with children, representing more than 22 million children in 11 million homes, keep at least one gun in the house. Nearly all childhood unintentional shooting deaths occur in or around the home. Fifty percent occur in the home of the victim, and nearly 40 percent occur in the home of a friend or relative." "The gun of choice is a handgun. Unintentional shootings seem to occur outside of school when children are unsupervised (4 to 5 p.m., weekends, summer months, and holidays)" (www.preventinjury.com).

Staggering statistics from the Children's Defense Fund indicate that "the number of children killed by guns in 2006 would fill more than 127 public school classrooms of 25 students each. More preschoolers were killed by firearms than law enforcement officers killed in the line of duty. Since 1979, gun violence has ended the lives of 107,603 children and teens in America." The sad part about this is that these numbers continue to rise every year. When will it stop?

One in three black boys and one in six Latino boys born in 2001 are at risk of going to prison in their lifetime. Boys are five times more likely to go to prison than girls; however the number of girls in the juvenile system is on the rise dramatically. We have to begin changing our education system so that children and teenagers do not enter the pipeline to prison or early death. How will we do this?

We can begin by treating youths at risk as potentially productive members of society, instead of lost causes in prison cages. We need to empower children to have a vision of their future and the role they play in those goals being attained. Everyone in America needs to have the possibility of being successful, productive and happy.

It is essential that communities begin establishing community-based alternatives to detention. Youths at risk need to be looked at individually and receive individualized and developmentally appropriate services and direction. There has to be better collaboration between all the agencies who service this population. Improving collaboration with mental health agencies, as well as the child welfare system, the juvenile justice system, and education professionals, would go a long way in improving these long-standing problems.

The system of care needs to be ongoing and follow up with these youths so that once they are back on the streets they can function as productive members of society and not become a returning visitor to the juvenile correction system.

M. Rosenbach indicated in her 2001 report of the State Children's Health Insurance Program that there were 9 to 10 million uninsured children in America. The numbers have now increased so that there are more like 12 to 13 million children without insurance. "Every 39 seconds a child is born uninsured, meaning that more than 2200 children are born every day uninsured." The number of children enrolled in the State Children's Health Insurance Program is approximately 7 million. There are over 32 million children enrolled in Medicaid. "Child enrollment accounts for over 49 percent of all people enrolled in Medicaid, yet medical expenditures for children only account for about 22 percent of total Medicaid expenditures." Our health care system is in crisis.

The present system is extremely complicated, very expensive, and often unattainable to families who are barely surviving in their daily lives. Our challenge is to get health care to those who need it the most. Can we really afford to have a whole generation of children and teenagers who are not receiving adequate health care? Congress has made movement toward universal health care; however there is still a ways to go so that the children of this country will be properly served and taken care of in a meaningful way.

Education in the United States is also in crisis. School districts do not have the money to adequately fund programs, salaries, and services. The amount spent per pupil in public schools is around eight thousand dollars per student. This amount varies according to state. "The percent of public school fourth graders performing below grade level in reading is about 68 percent nationwide and in math it is 61 percent" (Children's Defense Fund 2009).

Why are our schools failing? What do we need to do to infuse a layer of professionalism and success? Is it by better teacher education programs at the higher education institutions? Is it by dumping more money? Is it time to overhaul the system as it stands? Why is the rest of the world progressing while America, which is often seen as a leader in education, is falling behind or invested in keeping the status quo?

We have become better aware of how children learn, how they develop, how the brain works, how to improve methodology, and yet our school systems remain in crisis. What needs to be done? Is it time to become completely individual student directed and abandon the system as it now exists? The investigation and data collection needs to continue; however, we need to stop ignoring the problems and move toward change and solutions that will revolutionize how we do business in our public schools.

The child welfare system is also in chaos in this country. The number of children who are victims of abuse and neglect tops over 900,000 (U.S. Department of Commerce 2008). "If we break down the abuse by category, Neglect and Medical Neglect account for 73 percent of all cases. Physical Abuse is about 16 percent and Sexual Abuse is 9.5 to 10 percent. Psychological and other maltreatment is about 15 percent" (National Data Archive on Child Abuse 2007).

"The number of children in foster care is over 500,000. Their average length of stay in foster care is about 27.2 months" (Children's Bureau AF-CARS Report 2008). "Research indicates that if a child or youth is in two or fewer placements, the likelihood of them remaining there less than 12 months is about 84 percent. The more placements the child or youth has, the odds that the placements will be longer and more than 24 months is about 32 percent." These numbers are staggering. Why are there so many children in crisis?

The reasons are that their parents and their communities are in crisis. Adults in their lives can barely look after themselves and yet are charged with looking after their children. Many do not have the capacity or means to be parents but obviously do become parents.

The number of grandparents raising their grandchildren is almost 3 million individuals. This in itself is becoming part of the national norm. In the past, it was rare to see grandparents becoming the primary caretakers, but now in some communities it is a very normal and accepted part of life. Grandparents, instead of looking forward to retirement, are now being asked to raise a second family, in many circumstances without adequate financial means.

"Of the many children who end up in foster care (500,000), only about 50,000 ever get adopted permanently into a home, so where do the others go?" Who looks after them? How many of these 500,000 end up in our jails and in the streets? (yourbloodismyblood.blogspot.com).

"Youths at risk in the United States do not graduate from high school. The national dropout rate is anywhere from 6.7 percent to 30 percent in some communities. Youths who do not graduate from high school also have a 15 to 20 percent unemployment rate." The environment is now ripe for crime.

The number of juvenile arrests last year in this country was almost 1.3 million youths (www.schoolsystem.org).

These youths end up in either jail or residential facilities and account for huge tax burdens on certain states and communities. It is almost 2.8 times more expensive to keep a youth in jail than it is to keep them in school. If we look at the situation from a financial point of view we know we need to keep them going to school until they can graduate and find employment. The one way to do so is to revamp what youths learn and do in high schools. The high schools of America need to become more progressive and match the needs of their clients.

Now that I have completely shattered any of your ideals about American society and how it treats its youngest participants, it is important to remember that we are not helpless, we can effect change. We can begin by protecting children. We can educate parents. We can empower teachers. We can motivate lawmakers and politicians. We can begin one child at a time.

2

Juvenile Sex Offenders

What makes a juvenile want to sexually offend other children or youths? Someone so young with this kind of pathology is a concern. Parents and educators do not have a sense of what this psychopathology is all about. Many cannot fathom an adolescent sexually offending when their own sexuality is just developing and opening up. How can they be a sexual deviant already? There is very little information available to the general public, which means that people are generally not aware or informed.

Sex offenders are youths that commit a sex offense. "A sex offender is defined as a person convicted of one of the following sex offenses: Sexual assault in the first, second or third degree; Unlawful sexual contact; Sexual assault on a child; Incest; Sexual exploitation of children; Pimping of a child; Inducement of child prostitution" (www.familywatchdog.us/laws/COlaws.asp).

The age range of a sex offender usually ranges from when an individual begins puberty and reaches legal adult (age of majority); for many states this is eighteen years of age. In determining whether an assault is an offense against any person of any age, the courts consider whether it is against the victim's will, without consent, or in an aggressive or threatening manner. "The current politically correct term is 'Adolescent Responsible for Sexual Offense.' In some states, e.g. South Carolina, even pre-pubescent children can be classified as sex offender" (Koenigsburg 2008–2010).

"The majority of adolescents that engage in sexually harmful behaviors come from disrupted family systems, they have been the victims of sexual abuse, someone in the family has been sexually victimized and there has been a history of domestic violence and/or substance abuse in the home. This indicates that the sexually harmful behaviors have an ecological etiology and are developmental in nature" (Koenigsburg 2008–2010).

So what is a sexual offense in the eyes of the law in America? There are nontouching and touching offenses that have been defined so that the courts can have a list of criteria as to evaluate if there is an issue.

The nontouching offenses are:

1. Asking a child to touch someone else's private parts
2. Exposing oneself
3. Making obscene phone calls
4. Taking photos of a child for sexual purposes
5. Communicating with a child in a sexual way via email or the Internet and/or showing a child pornography (www.legalappeal. co.uk/3_DefinitionsofSexualOffences).

The touching offenses are:

1. Performing anal, oral, or vaginal sex on a child without their consent or under the age of consent
2. Forcing a child to perform sexual acts on another person
3. Touching a child in private areas of body or making a child touch private parts of another (www.legalappeal.co.uk/3_DefinitionsofSexual Offences).

When there is an investigation into a sexual offense because of suspicious actions or a child has reported an incident the process of investigation is initiated. The police will classify the acts in one of these two categories to begin with as a way to base what needs to be done in terms of protocols and procedures. Generally there are different consequences depending on the offense. In the past touching offenses have a tendency to have much stricter penalties and will result in automatic detention of the youth immediately. This is often used as a way to stop the offending or to protect the victims. Depending on the age of the youth, the investigating officers will ask for identification and if the possible offender is beyond 15 years of age, it usually results in the case and the youth offender being moved to adult court for prosecution.

Who are these offenders? The list of the most common characteristics is usually present in most of the juvenile sex offenders. A word of caution: not all juvenile sex offenders exhibit these characteristics with any level of predictability.

1. Most adolescent sex offenders come from two-parent homes.
2. Fewer than five percent have been previously diagnosed with a mental disorder.

3. They have a history of poor family functioning.
4. Alcohol or drug abuse by parents.
5. Poor impulse control.
6. Lack of self-esteem.
7. Poor social skills.
8. Deviant sexual interests.
9. A history of physical abuse, sexual abuse, neglect.
10. Family violence can be found in the background of most adolescent sex offenders.

Koenigsberg (2008–2010) in his research indicated that "over 50% of adolescent offenders report some parental loss, such as divorce, illness or death of a parent, adoption or temporary separations. Over 90% of adolescent sex offenders are male. Adolescent offenders perpetrate 50% of sex offenses against boys, and 15% to 20% of offenses against girls. Offenders under age 18 account for 17% of forced rape occurrences and 18% of other sex crimes, with the victims most often a younger female relative or acquaintance of the offender."

A juvenile offender is very manipulative in that he often uses control, persuasion, and a private environment to commit the offense. He manipulates the victim into thinking they instigated the sexual acts and that it was all their idea and of their own choosing. Offenders have been heard to say frequent. "Well they wanted to, I did not force them, they were willing participants." It is a well-known and researched fact that the offender almost always abuses someone significantly younger and who they know personally or are related to.

The following is a commonly used checklist to identify the profile of a juvenile sex offender. If there are six or more characteristics present in a young adolescent male, then careful observation of the youth's behavior is warranted.

CHARACTERISTICS OF JUVENILE SEX OFFENDERS

- Trust issues—they have difficulties trusting others
- Aberrant sexual fantasies
- Are not in touch with feelings (emotions)
- Difficulty in communicating needs and feelings
- Socially isolated and superficial relationships, lack of empathy, attachment issues
- Antisocial thoughts

- Control issues—want excessive control
- Impulse control difficulties
- Limited understanding about sexuality and low sexual skill level
- Underachievers that lack positive goals
- Think what they are doing is okay—denial or minimization
- Come from a dysfunctional family with poor or no personal boundaries— they do not understand the whole concept of appropriate personal boundaries (Koenigsberg 2008–2010).

RISK FACTORS

Here are some of the risk factors that have been identified in developing juvenile sexual offenders:

- Early exposure to pornography
- Lack of privacy in living environment
- Being either over- or under-sexualized
- Emotional incest
- Emotional abuse or neglect
- Feelings of abandonment
- Role models that use force to get their way
- Shame-based family functioning
- Exaggerated sexual talk
- Harassment, bullying
- Access to victims
- Aggression: gets in conflicts and fights a lot (Koenigsberg 2008–2010).

I would caution that having these risk factors does not necessarily make a young person an offender; however having these criteria will definitely highlight the possibility that the young individual may be more prone to offending.

There are seven sub-types of juvenile sex offenders. This list was compiled by Michael J. O'Brien and Walter H. Bera (1992).

1. Naïve Experimenter: this is the youth who is curious about sex and sexual behaviors and is generally a late developer.
2. Under-socialized Child Exploiter: this youth is often a loner, has very few social skills and wants to be connected to another child or youth but does not have the social cues to develop age appropriate relationships.

3. Pseudo-socialized Child Exploiter: this youth is very socially conscious and will use charm and skills to manipulate, lie, and trick children into sexual behaviors.
4. Sexually Aggressive: this youth has a very strong sexual appetite and is very aware of his own sexuality and drive. He will often use power and control to achieve the sexual exploitation. He will often plan his attacks.
5. Sexually Compulsive: this youth is motivated by obsessions with sex and pornography and is compelled to act frequently to satisfy an inner drive or need.
6. Disturbed-Impulsive: this youth suffers from past trauma and abuse and will on an impulse offend with inappropriate sexualized behaviors. It is more a spur of the moment action and is often done impulsively without planning.
7. Group Influenced: this youth is influenced by a group to take part in a sexual attack upon another youth or child. May offend as part of a ritual gang initiation, to prove his masculinity or prowess, and will take part in gang rapes. This type of offender often will use alcohol and drugs as a precursor to offending.

Depending on the level of the cognitive development, maturity, life experiences, and/or history of the offender, they may engage in the following types of denial that sex offenders might experience:

1. Many will deny the crime itself; they actually believe they have not done anything wrong or criminal. There is often a denial of responsibility for the crime: it was not their fault, someone made them do it, or the victim wanted the sexual act. They are unable to admit any type of accountability or responsibility.
2. There is denial of intent and premeditation: it is something that just happened and they could not stop it.
3. There is denial of injury to the victim because the victim really wanted to participate in the sexual acts and they were just giving the victim what he or she really wanted. Some actually believe that there is nothing wrong with one youth having sexualized behaviors and acts with another youth. It is only bad if an adult and a child have sexual relationships.
4. Many of these juvenile sex offenders deny the difficulty of change and the need for help: in their eyes they have done nothing wrong so why would they need treatment. It is part of the growing up experience.
5. They often will deny the frequency of the deviant acts as they have no recollection of how many times, or when, or the circumstances in

which the abuse or the offense took place. They seem unaware of the frequency, duration, and intensity of the actions. It is almost as if they have blocked it out and are unable to give adequate recounts of the offenses.

There is a continuum of denial for sexual offenders. There are four levels that are indicated on this continuum. Depending on the personality type, the level of previous trauma or abuse, the history, the numbers of characteristics present, and the risk factors, an offender will be at a specific stage of denial when first apprehended.

Level I: Minimal avoidance of responsibility: Admits that the offense occurred, but does not take full responsibility.

Level II: Moderate avoidance of responsibility: Admits to some of the behaviors, but justifies their occurrence and makes them seem less significant than they are.

Level III: Strongly avoids responsibility: Does not admit to a specific offense, but may admit to less harmful behaviors.

Level IV: Severely avoids responsibility: Completely denies the offense.

Depending on the level of denial the treatment path will be different. It is clearly articulated that the more avoidance of responsibility, the more likely there will be reoffending. The success rate of treatment will be dependent on getting the youth to accept responsibility for their actions. Not an easy task.

What can parents do to protect their children? Parents can help protect their children by teaching them awareness of dangerous people and the lures used to entice the children. Set aside time to talk to your child about dangerous people and strangers. Keep recent files on your children, such as: a recent photo, physical description, extra activities, friends' names, addresses and phone numbers.

Abductors usually select a child that they think will be an easy target. They look for children who walk alone to school, take shortcuts, or seem to be alienated from other children. Be cautious when selecting a person to care for your children, meet with them and check their references.

Recent research suggests that there are very distinct differences between juvenile and adult sexual offenders. There is not a predicable profile as every juvenile offender is very different. "There is little evidence to support the assumption that the majority of juvenile sexual offenders are destined to become adult sexual offenders. The significantly lower frequency of more extreme forms of sexual aggression, fantasy, and compulsivity among juveniles compared to adults, suggests that many juveniles have sexual behavior problems that may be more amenable to intervention" (Association for the Treatment of Sexual Abusers 2000). There seems to be more hope for the youth offender than an adult offender who has a history of repeated offenses or violating behaviors.

A series of research studies has indicated that, "In fact, recent prospective and clinical outcome studies suggest that many juveniles who sexually abuse will cease this behavior by the time they reach adulthood, especially if they are provided with specialized treatment and supervision." Research studies that have spent extensive amount of time studying juvenile offenders have discovered that many of these offenders "may be more responsive to treatment than their adult counterparts, due to their emerging development" (Association for the Treatment of Sexual Abusers 2000). There seems to be a period of time when identity, behavior, and personality can be shaped with the proper interventions.

The treatment of juvenile sex offenders has found lasting success and more positive results when there has been involvement of parents, caregivers, and family members. This is the difference with juvenile treatment outcomes and adult offender treatment where the family members often will distance themselves from the adult offender. These studies, "in addition to clinical observation, support the growing optimism that many juvenile sexual offenders can be successfully treated" (ATSA 2000).

JUVENILE SEX OFFENDERS WITH DEVELOPMENTAL DISABILITIES

Many communities struggle with the issue of managing adult sex offenders with developmental disabilities. Society and the justice system do not have a clear understanding of many developmental disabilities and are even more at a lost as to what to do when the offender is a juvenile. "Although they may be different in terms of their cognitive skills, developmentally disabled sex offenders pose many of the same challenges to supervision agencies as other adult or juvenile sex offenders" (CSOM 2007).

Many juvenile agencies want to treat juvenile sex offenders with developmental disabilities differently; however it is important to remember the following:

1. "Juvenile sex offenders with developmental disabilities pose as clear a threat to public safety as sex offenders without developmental disabilities." A juvenile sex offender is still a threat to the safety of the children in which he interacts with regardless of the disability.

2. "Developmental disabilities do not cause or excuse sexual offending." It is often easy to negate or discount the offense as the individual does not know any better or does not have the cognitive ability. Being of lower cognitive ability is not an excuse.
3. "Sex offenders with developmental disabilities should be provided treatment that is appropriate to their developmental capacity and their level of comprehension." It is imperative that proper treatment be given to all who offend (CSOM 2007).

To assess effectively whether a sex offender with developmental disabilities can be adequately managed in the community given the unique kinds of services they are likely to need, supervision and treatment agencies must:

1. "Evaluate the offender's level of cognitive impairment to gauge his or her suitability for community supervision." A very clear evaluation must be done to evaluate how responsive this developmentally individual can be to treatment but also the risk he or she may pose to the community. There has to be a very clear understanding by all involved in the case the extent of choice and control the individual has in controlling their behaviors.
2. "Work with treatment providers who are knowledgeable about sex offending behavior and have treated developmentally disabled individuals." You need to have very specialized and trained case managers who have a complete skill set around how to manage the disabilities that are manifested by the developmentally delayed individual.
3. "Work intensively with personnel from mental health and social services departments, group home staff, and others who may be involved closely in the offender's daily life." There has to be a complete wraparound model where everyone who is involved is on the same page and is consistent in the enforcement of the strategies and interventions" (CSOM 2007).

The assessment of possible offenders is not a clear science and must be monitored consistently and frequently. The assessment must be ongoing and clinicians need to be well trained.

TREATMENT

At the outset, there are four basics involved in the treatment of juvenile sex offenders:

- "Sexual offenders in general are not very responsive to therapeutic intervention." Years of research have shown that there is no magic bullet. No program or therapeutic treatment has had long-lasting results. Research in these interventions has had very discouraging results.
- "Early intervention is key and the greater the chance of success." The goal is to catch them early so that there can be behavioral training that can lead the offender to making different choices. The longer the delay in the treatment the less likely is success.
- "The goal in therapy in many cases is not to 'cure' the offender, but rather to protect society from them." There is no cure, just management strategies.
- "A guiding principle is deterrence: the consequence imposed by society for molesting, assaulting, or abusing others, is that they will go to jail." If we lock them up they will not offend; however, the threat of jail is not enough of a deterrent to prevent the offending. Sometimes incarceration is the only solution. Koenigsburg 2008–2010).

Treatment usually involves both group and individual therapy. "In group therapy, other offenders are good at recognizing lies and deceits. This is similar to addicts recognizing the ploys of other addicts. As a result, the best addiction counselors are those that are recovering addicts" (Koenigsburg 2008–2010).

In most treatment programs or leveled interventions juvenile sex offenders are taught social skills and what the norms of that society are. There is an expectation that the offender be able to understand and abide by these societal expectations. Cognitive distortions are explored and given voice. Often time therapists are flabbergasted by the deranged thinking that comes out of these youth offenders. The majority of programs will focus on building anger management, communication skills, and listening skills. Problem solving skills are enhanced—at least these are the goals of therapy (Koenigsberg 2008–2010).

The Association for the Treatment of Sexual Abusers (ATSA) tries to promote a high-quality, juvenile-specific, community-based treatment that would be mandated for juvenile sexual offenders. They have chosen as a mission a program that hopefully will lead to change for these young offenders. They question and have found very troubling the fact that many courts are imposing adult sentences for the majority of the juvenile sexual offenders. The placements of juveniles in adult jails have all kinds of psychological and physical ramifications. The association believes that "incarcerating juveniles in adult correctional settings may restrict their access to treatment, expose them to the potentially detrimental influences of anti-social adult role models, as well as create management and safety issues" (ATSA 2000).

ATSA believes "that most juvenile sexual offenders can be safely and effectively managed in the community if they receive specialized treatment and court supervision." Many childrens rights organizations have challenged this belief and stated that the ATSA is naïve and foolish in these beliefs. These young offenders are dangerous and need to be removed from community living.

ATSA indicated that any type of treatment that occurs in the community occurs after a very comprehensive assessment "that allows for the tailoring and titration of interventions based upon the risks presented by the juvenile offender." The fact that the young offender is in the community "recognizes that community-based treatment also offers opportunities for family involvement in the treatment process as well as reintegration into productive community roles (e.g., student, employee, family member)." This support network may lead to more rapid gains in the treatment.

They are not naïve in their approaches because they also recognize "that some juveniles require treatment in a structured, secure residential program due to the severity of their psychosexual and psychiatric problems." Not all offenders can be treated successfully in a home community–based program. It is the reality of the psychological disorder.

ATSA recommends "that sanctions which best serve the long-term interests of the community and the juvenile be considered and that those who make the final decisions have access to a broad range of potential sanctions and placement options." A decision be made that is best for all and that there not be a cookie cutting process to intervention. Each individual be thoroughly evaluated and that the best program be chosen based on these individual needs, behaviors and cognitive levels.

It is also the belief of ATSA that juveniles "should be subject to community notification procedures in only the most extreme cases." This type of thinking is controversial in that many community members want to know if there is an offender living in their midst. These community members believe it is their right to protect their children in that neighborhood.

There is no set way how communities interpret and implement notification laws. In the case of adult offenders the process is well established and communities are informed. Young offenders and their locations are often not published as a matter of public record. In some states notification is restricted to the immediate area in which the adolescent resides, ignoring their ability to move beyond these limited geographic boundaries.

In some parts of America the implementation of community notification varies from jurisdiction to jurisdiction even within an individual state. Many communities argue that there are benefits of community notification with juveniles, while others indicate that it is a well-known fact that "this public knowledge will stigmatize the adolescent, fostering peer rejection, isolation, increased anger, and consequences for the juvenile's family members" (ATSA 2000). This will either lead to violence against the family or the individual juvenile offender.

ATSA believes that "until research has demonstrated the protective efficacy of notification with juveniles and explored the impact of notification on the youth, their families and the community, notification—if imposed at all for juveniles—should be done conscientiously, cautiously, and selectively." The issue of notification is still very contentious and will continue to be a point of discussion until societies figure out how to effectively deal with this type of social issue and offender. We as a society still have issues wrapping our thinking about kids who hurt other kids. It is not supposed to happen.

In the last several years all states have enacted sex offender registration laws as a means of providing law enforcement with an additional investigative tool. Police and juvenile offending departments now have the ability to track and collect data on juvenile offenders who have either been convicted, identified, or incarcerated in an institution.

To achieve these goals, states have developed numerous promising approaches to sex offender registration. These include:

1. Developing written policies and procedures detailing the registration process,
2. Collecting thorough information on registered sex offenders,
3. Providing ready access to this information for all law enforcement officers, and
4. Developing systems to transfer registration information within and across state lines effectively and efficiently (CSOM 2007).

The Adam Walsh Child Protection and Safety Act of 2006 requires:

1. The further integration of information of state sex offender registry systems
2. That law enforcement will have access to the same information across the United States
3. All 50 states to enact sex offender community notification laws. The reasoning behind these laws is to ensure that the public can access information that will assist them in protecting themselves and their families from known dangerous sex offenders who reside in their communities.

ATSA notes "that juveniles should be held legally accountable for their behavior. Such accountability is necessary to assist the offender in taking responsibility for their offending behavior, to ensure compliance with therapeutic requirements, and to address the needs of the victim." Accountability is needed at all levels of the process. It must be done with a level of consistency and must be applicable to the individual case.

The adjudication process of juvenile sex offenders needs to be managed by clinicians with specialized training in working with this population who have experience doing this type of evaluations. An inexperienced clinician could make serious misdiagnosis mistakes that would then put community children at risk. A trained clinician should be able to gather a series of facts and evidence whereas these evaluations could determine if the juvenile is amenable to treatment and to assist the court in identifying the most appropriate type and level of care.

Treatment needs to be court ordered and be based on solid evaluations that have been rigorous in their collection. Evidence put forth by the ATSA suggests "that the vast majority of juvenile sexual offenders respond well to treatment and do not recidivate. Most juvenile sexual offenders can be safely and effectively treated in the community, if they are provided with specialized treatment and on-going court supervision" (2010). The evidence is quite conclusive and has shown accurate results when treatment and assessment have been done early and effectively.

The assessment of juvenile sex offenders must be comprehensive in any type of treatment plan. There cannot be any type of randomness to this process because of the complex and varying nature of sexual abuse and the individuals who perpetrate it. Anyone who works with juvenile sex offenders as a practitioner must assess their behavior effectively and in an ongoing, collaborative fashion. A single practitioner may be likely to be manipulated and/or controlled by the juvenile sex offender. Working collaboratively decreases the likelihood of this manipulation.

Teams of practitioners are more likely to have similar findings in their assessment and therefore manage the different levels of risk that offenders pose overtime to victims and the community. This commonality in assessment will results in more effective interventions or placements. "Sex offender assessment can be seen as a process that has two related domains (risk and clinical) and interdependent purposes, which practitioners must understand and communicate about clearly and consistently" (CSOM 2007).

The risk assessment domain has two purposes: risk prediction and risk management. "Risk prediction is the science of estimating the likelihood of recidivism over a period of years" (CSOM 2007). It has been reported with consistency that assessment tools that have been well researched and tested over time enhance the ability of practitioners to identify subgroups of offenders who pose a higher risk to re-offend than others.

"Risk management is the process (undertaken by probation/parole officers, treatment providers, police officers, victim advocates, and many others) of recognizing and responding to ongoing, short-term (hourly, daily, or weekly) changes in sex offender risk" (CSOM 2007).

This process is based on the premise and assumptions that every sex offender has a unique set of dynamic and personality factors that are as individual as their individual personality. These factors can also speak to the type of immediate risk they pose. Research suggests that there are specific, changeable factors that should be monitored over time. It is key to remember that one must not generalize but individualize when dealing with juvenile sex offenders.

The clinical assessment domain also has two purposes: clinical diagnosis and clinical treatment planning. "Clinical diagnosis is the process of assessing whether psychological, psychiatric, or psycho-sexual problems are present in sex offenders" (CSOM 2007).

The results will often impact whether the criminal justice process becomes the course of action or another determination of appropriate treatment responses occurs as a result of an effective assessment that has led to a clinical diagnosis that may include mental health or pathology issues.

Clinical treatment planning includes: "the assessment of sex offenders' specific treatment needs and the development of comprehensive treatment plans that respond to these needs; the ongoing assessment of these needs; and the effectiveness of the treatment interventions employed (treatment progress)" (CSOM 2007). It becomes paramount that this process of evaluation is done with a level of confidence and fidelity.

At any point in time when doing any type of work or assessment with juvenile sex offenders it is important that "the information garnered from risk prediction tools; risk management, clinical diagnosis, and clinical treatment processes inform the critically important point-in-time and ongoing decisions that practitioners make throughout the criminal justice process (beginning at arrest and ending at the termination of a sentence) to protect victims and the community" (CSOM 2007).

Juvenile sex offenders are members of this society and are part of every community across America. The goal is to identify what happens in these individuals during their childhood that creates a desire to hurt others. The psychology of the juvenile sex offender is fascinating in that we have much research to do to truly understand all the complex natures of this population.

We can identify, support, treat and incarcerate; the real solution is to prevent them from developing in the first place. What is it in society that creates them? There will be more of them created over the next few years. The search continues for the answers.

3

Juvenile Sociopaths and Serial Killers

What is a sociopath? Many teachers and parents do not have a clue as to what constitutes a real juvenile sociopath. Below is a list of criteria that will clarify for the reader exactly what to look for when working with this type of youth.

This type of youth has also been known as a psychopath or antisocial personality disorder or sociopathic personality disorder. These are the clinical diagnosis or labels based on a series of criteria: They are often diagnosed in their late teens and early 20s. There is a direct correlation between children with conduct disorder (40 to 70 percent). They are often seen as very callous, deceitful, reckless, guiltless, often intimidating, and sometimes violent.

CAUSES OF SOCIOPATHIC BEHAVIOR IN CHILDREN

Personality develops in childhood; it is shaped through heredity (genetic vulnerability) and environment (life situations trigger disorder). The causes of antisocial behavior in children may range from abnormal development of the nervous system to certain genetic factors. Here is a list of causes for the development of sociopathic tendencies in children retrieved from www.buzzle.com.

Hereditary Basis: Sometimes children may inherit the sociopathic behavioral symptoms from the parents. Research has shown that children who are adopted and have sociopathic biological parents can display the characteristics of this psychological illness.

Physiological Basis: Researchers believe that abnormalities in the development of the nervous system may result in learning disorders, hyperactivity and persistent bedwetting. In addition to this research, certain brain imaging studies have found that abnormal brain functioning may result in sociopathic behavior in children. While the serotonin (neurotransmitter) has been linked with impulsive and aggressive behavior, the prefrontal cortex and the temporal lobes in the brain help regulate mood and behavior. Dysfunctional or abnormal serotonin levels in these brain regions may result in antisocial behavior in children.

Environmental Basis: The home environment or alcoholic parents may also contribute to the child developing these tendencies. Inappropriate disciplinary techniques or inadequate emotional bonding with the parents can also result in children displaying sociopathic behavior. At times the death of a parent, an accident, or other traumatic events can trigger of the sociopathic tendencies.

The above categories need to be developed much further when looking at the cause of antisocial behavior patterns.

There are several risk factors that seem to be common to all youths who are sociopaths:

1. Childhood conduct disorder
2. Family history of ASPD or mental illness
3. Being subjected to verbal, physical or sexual abuse during childhood
4. Having an unstable or chaotic family life during childhood
5. Loss of parents (death or traumatic divorce) during childhood (American Psychiatric Association 2000; American Psychiatric Association 2008; Duggan 2009).

The American Psychiatric Association (2000; 2008) has also put together a list of diagnostic criteria for youths who may be identified as sociopathic:

- At least 18 years old
- Having had symptoms of conduct disorder before age 15, which may include such acts as stealing, vandalism, violence, cruelty to animals, and bullying
- Repeatedly breaking the law
- Repeatedly conning or lying to others
- Being irritable and aggressive, repeatedly engaging in physical fights or assaults
- Feeling no remorse, or justifying behavior, after harming others
- Having no regard for the safety of self or others
- Acting impulsively and not planning ahead

Many of the youths who are sociopaths are found in our school system and their behaviors are often identified early as being difficult children or acting out or aggressive children. Some of the behaviors are identified early on even in preschool. The behaviors are often frequent and have intensity early on. These youths are often identified early because of the extreme of their behaviors in certain situations.

The behaviors seem to escalate throughout middle and high school. The following behaviors have often been attributed to youths who become sociopaths. This list is not exhaustive but a great beginning to making adults and educators more aware.

- Disregard for right and wrong
- Persistent lying or deceit
- Using charm or wit to manipulate others
- Recurring difficulties with the law
- Repeatedly violating the rights of others
- Child abuse or neglect
- Intimidation of others
- Aggressive or violent behavior
- Lack of remorse about harming others
- Impulsive behavior
- Agitation
- Poor or abusive relationships
- Irresponsible work behavior
- High drop-out rate
- Difficulty relating with peers
- Social isolation
- Anxiety and depression (American Psychiatric Association 2000; American Psychiatric Association 2008; Hesse 2010).

Because many of them do not have successful school experiences they become a burden to the existing school system that they are in. They become even more rebellious in their actions. They challenge more and more the status quo and become more aggressive. It is during the middle and high school years that many of them either get expelled from their neighborhood schools or find themselves in trouble with the law enforcement officials.

The life implications for many of these youth are not favorable or promising. Many of them become ward of the state or are part of the juvenile justice system. There is a very high incarceration with high recidivism. Once in the system they continually act out and offend regularly. They do not seem to learn from their mistakes. At times the level of aggression becomes more and more elevated where many are jailed for years.

Alcohol and substance abuse becomes a daily routine. It is as if they are trying to numb themselves from the realities of their life and circumstances. Part of the usage is due to peer pressure but it is my belief that it is a way of coping with the ugliness of their actions and how rotten their quality of life is, it may simply be a way of escaping.

Abuse is often very frequent in their backgrounds. Many were abused as children because of their acting and defiant behaviors. They are not easy and compliant children. They are often very rude and aggressive and challenge adult authority frequently, resulting in very harsh discipline measures being used as a way to control them.

As youths and young adults they become abusers toward weaker children or other youth which they perceive as being weaker. They become the bullies and the aggressors. They use violence and intimidation as a way to manipulate and control their followers or the people in their lives. Either way, the cycle of abuse continues, often with tragic results.

Reckless behavior, risky sexual behavior, gambling problems, and suicidal behavior are all part of the profile of this youth life circumstances. They engage in these outrageous behaviors as a way of feeling alive. It seems that the riskier it is the better the thrill. They seem to have a sense that their lives may be cut short so they live life very fast and take what they can.

There is a lack of stability; they often do not have a permanent residence and float from home to home or couch to couch. They do not have an address so they are hard to track down. If they qualify for any type of assistance they often can't be found to receive it.

Anxiety and depression are part of their regular mental health lives. Many have unresolved issues that prevent them from normal cognitive processing and problem solving. They have cognitive distortions based on their experiences that guide their choices and decisions. This is why so many make bad decisions and are involved in all the trouble or dysfunctional activity that comes their way.

Relationship difficulties are at the forefront of their experiences. They have never had positive role models and do not have a point of reference of what it is like to be in a functional and healthy relationship. They have only seen the dysfunction within their homes or the lack of skill on the part of their parents so they cannot begin to demonstrate positive behaviors while in a relationship. Their relationships are often based on power, control and intimidation.

Social isolation is very common because of their inadequate social skills. They are not liked by their peers because their peers fear them. Their peers are afraid of the acting behaviors and the threats that have come their way in past interactions. They just choose to avoid thus fueling more anger and isolation on the part of the sociopathic youth.

School and work problems are very common as many of these youths do not have the skills to follow through and complete tasks. They give up quickly and will act out to distract or reject adults that are trying to make the youth more accountable. They can't keep a job because they do not have the required work ethic to be successful. They do not want to begin at the bottom; they want the compensation without having done the work.

They have strained relationships with health care providers because the individuals are seen as controlling and to be avoided as they are trying to restrict their freedom or actions. These youth are often very good at escaping or avoiding these health care workers because of the fear of being locked up in a mental health facility. It is better to be free so many of these at-risk youth do not get the mental health services they truly need.

These youth can become swindlers, thieves, cult leaders, nonviolent child molesters, corrupt businessmen, demagogic politicians, gangsters, armed robbers, rapists, and professional killers, so as you can see, the prognosis is not promising. They seem to find a place in society but often a place of dysfunction and violence. They embark on a life of crime, aggression, and possibly destruction of others (American Psychiatric Association 2000; American Psychiatric Association 2008; *Harvard Mental Health Letter* 2000; Hesse 2010).

Treatment options are very tricky. Below is a list of possible interventions. They are often excluded from treatment because they are rejected by therapists who either fear for their safety or are not trained properly to deal and guide this type of youth. The key is to find a therapist who can manage, manipulate and have shared power and control with the youth.

Parents often don't believe their child needs to change, as they think their son is perfectly normal and does not need help. The key is to inform parents about the dysfunctional behavior and to show evidence of the abnormal behaviors in a way that the parent will not become defensive and will want to cooperate to help their child learn new behaviors.

Few treatments have actually been developed that have been proven successful in the long run. Treatments are more effective when used to target the symptoms (substance abuse, DUI, anger, violence).

Psychotherapy such as the following has had limited success:

1. Cognitive behavioral approach (uncover negative and replace with positive)
2. Psychodynamic psychotherapy (raise awareness of unconscious thoughts and behaviors)

3. Psycho-education (coping strategies and problem-solving skills)
4. Stress and anger management skills for self and family
5. Medications for conditions sometimes associated with ASPD (antidepressants, mood-stabilizers, antianxiety, antipsychotics)
6. Hospitalization and residential treatment programs

The key to these types of interventions is to do it as early as possible. Early interventions during the early years are keys to teaching new behavior and coping skills. Often what happens is that services or supports are not given till the youth is an adolescent with very well entrenched behaviors that the youth has no intention of changing or modifying because these skills get him or her exactly what they want. By age twelve to thirteen it is often too late to change behaviors.

The goal of any adult who works with this population is to do the following in any type of intervention program or interaction. Every interaction between adult and youth gives you the opportunity to focus on doing one of these actions. It is only with repeated exposure will the youth begin internalizing the skills in their repertoire of skills and actions.

1. Teach decision-making skills.
2. Teach children to think before they act.
3. Teach problem-solving skills.
4. Teach ways to gain self-control.
5. Teach students about consequences.

The goal of any type of behavior support plan is to highlight the development of the following goals and objectives. The following have been proven as effective and realistic goals and objectives:

The student will make decisions appropriate to the situation.
The student will demonstrate self-control.
The student will consider consequences of his/her behavior.
The student will refrain from reacting impulsively.
The student will demonstrate behaviors that will result in positive consequences.
The student will follow school rules.
The student will interact appropriately with his/her peers (Vasil 2000).

Obviously it is important for the adults or team developing these behavior support plans to be aware of the individual characteristics of the youth at risk. These goals and objectives are a formula to begin developing effective plans to give this at-risk youth the necessary skills to become a fully integrated member of society. Not all youth will require the same plan so cookie cutting behavior support plans should not be in existence because of the uniqueness of the dysfunction exhibited by each individual youth.

In conclusion, if this type of at-risk youth is identified early and receives the correct type of interventions and training they can be turned around and become fully functioning productive members of their society. The lack of appropriate interventions leads to the creation of a disordered, criminally insane individual who may become so dysfunctional that he becomes a serial killer.

YOUTH AS A SERIAL KILLER

What creates a juvenile serial killer? The list is long and complex and there does not seem to be a natural route to this type of behavior or outrageous criminal actions. The FBI defines serial killing as three or more separate events in three or more separate locations with an emotional cooling off period between homicides. This definition stresses three elements:

1. Quantity: There have to be at least three murders
2. Place: The murders have to occur at different locations
3. Time: There has to be a cooling-off period, an interval between the murders that can last anywhere from several hours to several years (Federal Bureau of Investigation 2008).

Youth who become serial killers have a very troubled childhood often full of abuse, intimidation and horrendous experiences overall. However, some of these individuals have had reasonably normal childhoods so one must be careful not to overgeneralize the characteristics of this type of youth.

Here is a list of the most common traits of serial killers.

1. Most are single, white males.
2. They tend to be smart, with a mean IQ of "bright normal."
3. Despite their intelligence, they do poorly in school, have spotty employment records, and generally end up as unskilled workers.
4. They come from deeply troubled families. Typically, they have been abandoned at an early age by their fathers and grow up in broken homes dominated by their mothers.
5. There is a long history of psychiatric problems, criminal behavior, and alcoholism in their families.

6. As children, they suffer significant abuse—sometimes psychological, sometimes physical, often sexual. Such brutal mistreatment instills them with profound feelings of humiliation and helplessness.
7. Because of their resentment toward their distant, absent, or abusive fathers, they have a great deal of trouble with male authority figures. Because they were dominated by their mothers, they have a powerful hostility toward women.
8. They manifest psychiatric problems at an early age and often spend time in institutions as children.
9. Because of their extreme social isolation and a general hatred of the world and everyone in it (including themselves), they often feel suicidal as teenagers.
10. They display a precocious and abiding interest in deviant sexuality and are obsessed with fetishism, voyeurism, and violent pornography (twistedminds.creativescapism.com/psychological-disorders/).

There seems to be a commonality of experience in youths that do become serial killers as adults. There are three behavioral red flags. They are:

1. Bed-Wetting: "There's nothing unusual or alarming about bed-wetting in itself. It's a common phenomenon among little children. When the problem persists into puberty, however, it may well be a sign of significant and even dangerous emotional disturbance."
2. Fire Setting: "Given their list for destruction, it's no surprise that, among their other twisted pleasures, many serial killers love to set fires. A practice they often begin at an early age. Some of the most notorious serial killers of modern times were juvenile arsonists."
3. Animal Torture: Jeffrey Dahmer said, "I found a dog and cut it open just to see what the insides looked like, and for some reason I thought it would be a fun prank to stick the head on a stake and set it out in the woods." "Juvenile sadism directed at lower life-forms is nothing new. There have always been children and adolescents (usually male) who enjoy hurting small creatures. The cruelties, perpetrated by incipient serial killers, grow more extreme over time, until they are targeting not stray animals and house pets but other human beings. For them, animal torture isn't a stage. It's a rehearsal" (twistedminds.creativescapism. com/psychological-disorders/).

"Killer kids" who commit mass murder have become an all-too-common feature of contemporary American society. Serial murder perpetrated by minors is an exceptionally rare phenomenon. The most famous case in American history is that of Jesse Harding Pomeroy, the Boston "Boy Fiend," whose criminal career began when he was twelve. Though Pomeroy began torturing children when he was twelve, he didn't graduate to homicide until he was fourteen, which makes Craig Price of Warwick, Rhode Island, the youngest serial killer in U.S. history.

Many youths who become serial killers once into adulthood have had horrible childhood experiences that have left them with a twisted sense of what intimacy and sex is all about. It goes without saying that serial killers tend to have extraordinarily aberrant sex lives.

Their brutalized upbringings render them incapable of experiencing anything resembling real love. Many of them are impotent under normal conditions. They can only get aroused when they have another human being in their absolute power—a helpless, terrified object to be tortured, debased, slaughtered, and perhaps violated after death.

"Lacking any capacity for empathy or guilt, serial killers are unconstrained by the inhibitions that keep other people from acting out their darkest fantasies." To these psychopaths, there is nothing forbidden, nothing taboo. "They exist in a realm beyond the bounds not only of civilized behavior but even of ordinary criminal behavior. As a result, they indulge in activities that most people would find not just incomprehensible but inconceivable" (Schechter 2003).

So why do they kill? There have been many explanations over time; some have been very credible, others outlandish and from the source of an overcreative or imaginative author. The science of identifying why they kill is ongoing. The following have been identified as possible sources:

1. Atavism
2. Brain damage
3. Child abuse
4. Mother hate
5. Bad seed
6. Mean genes
7. Adoption
8. Fantasy
9. Bad books, malignant movies, vile videos
10. Pornography
11. Profit
12. Celebrity
13. Copycats
14. The devil made them do it (Schechter 2003).

Below is a short explanation of each one of these characteristics.

Atavism refers to the ancient, ancestral trait that reappears in modern life. Serial killers seem like barbaric and cannibalistic opportunists because of their history. The argument is that these individuals have suffered a complete breakdown of the normal socialization process. During childhood they were not able to get the necessary skills to develop morals, empathy and conscience and these skills were replaced with an animalistic primitive level of functioning. This may be why these monsters seem to evolve in our modern-day society.

There has been some evidence that serial killer brains are different and that many of the known serial killers all experienced some sort of head injury or trauma in their early years. Oftentimes the head trauma is directly caused by direct child maltreatment or abuse. The brain damage coupled with the emotional and psychological damage inflicted by a shockingly abusive upbringing creates a youth predisposed to becoming a serial killer.

Abuse creates a new type of child and youth. This child or youth has a malignant view of life. This child having been tortured by caretakers in the early years results in a youth who understands human relationships to be based in power, suffering and humiliation. These youth as they age seek out other individuals that they can control, torture, and inflict pain upon, almost as a way of getting revenge for the way they were treated as young children. However, not all youth who are abused become serial killers; severe child abuse may not be a sufficient cause in the creation of serial murderers but it appears to be a necessary one.

Mother hate is a result of mother-son relationships that are based in abuse. There is no doubt that several psychopathic serial killers grow up with a murderous rage against their mothers which they later target and kill women. They project their hate for their mother onto a certain type of female and begin killing them as a way of getting even with their mothers.

The bad seed argument is that some kids are just born evil and remain that way no matter what kind of childhood or parental experience they have. There has not been any evidence that a serial killer has come from a happy healthy home, all of them have been products of dysfunctional backgrounds.

Mean genes seem to come from research that is based on the fact that some children inherit certain types of genetic factors that when coupled with severe childhood maltreatment grow up to be criminally violent at a far higher rate than other children. It seems very likely that both nurture and nature play a role in the development of a potential serial killer.

Adoption has been a surprisingly common factor as many famous serial killers have been raised in adoptive or foster homes. Many of these serial killers have been children of prostitutes. The type of adoptive family can be the source of the development of their antisocial and pathologic personality. The more dysfunctional the adoptive or foster family the more the youth develops ways of coping that become unnatural or even perverse.

Fantasy is where the serial killer gets to live out all of his actions and he is able to plan his actions in a very safe area well within his brain. He will replay the fantasies till they become unbearable and he must act upon them to release the pressure. These fantasies begin very early and are often based in some sort of sadism, mass murder or revenge. As they reach puberty the fantasies turn sexual and are more about power and dominance, pain and degradation. What happens at this stage is that the youth wants to transform the fantasy into reality. Many of them have a tenuous hold on reality. Their fantasies become the fuel for murder.

Killer fantasy is hard to pinpoint unless the youth writes or speaks them out verbally. These dark fantasies sometimes are manifested in school by art or journal writings. The majority of these fantasies never see the light of day because the youth knows that verbalizing them will get him known and in trouble.

Bad books, malignant movies, and vile videos have all been blamed as the source of influence for these youths. The truth is that many individuals are exposed to all kinds of literature and media and they do not become serial killers. It does happen that a youth becomes obsessed with a movie and or a book but this alone is the not the cause of the acting out. It may influence the youth to think about certain aspects of serial murder but is not the catalyst to act out.

Pornography is often blamed but as is commonly known many law-abiding citizens have porn collections and they are totally normal in their behaviors. Pornography is often found within the homes of serial killers; it is said to play a part in the development of their fantasies. Very few serial killers have learned the tricks of their trade by watching porn. The influence of porn seems to be during the teenage years as an outlet for sexual frustration and fantasy.

It has become a huge debate as to whether serial killers should profit from the sale of their stories to media and movie business. This group looks for opportunities to profit off their actions. They are often media hounds looking for attention. Many of them kill for profit but also for their twisted pleasure.

They also become serial killers to gain celebrity and a place in history, to become famous. In fact they become infamous and do get a place in history but often one that is based in horrific situations and circumstances. Many of them will continue to kill and manipulate the press and police departments for years so that their reputation is guaranteed in American history.

Copycats are created when an individual has become famous due to his horrendous actions. This individual copies similar crimes in the hope of becoming famous or getting a feeling of self-importance. He will often re-search thoroughly a famous individual and will create a new identity that will surpass the original serial killer as a way of proving that he is better than the previous serial killer.

The devil made me do it explanation seems to be grounded in demonic pos-session or some sort of spiritual connection with higher powers. This excuse has not been seen in a court of law for many decades; it usually resulted in some sort of mental health diagnosis.

There have been several studies that have looked at the causes of why cer-tain mental health disorders or pathology develops in certain types of youth. Below you will find a summary of a variety of peer-reviewed research that correlated facts that cognitive and behavioral effects are linked to toxic metal exposure and resulting metabolic imbalances, including learning disabilities, ADD, violent prone and sociopathic behavior, juvenile delinquency, crimi-nality, and mass murder.

The full peer-reviewed research study references quoted below can be re-trieved at www.home.earthlink.net/~berniew1/damspr4.html.

The majority of the referenced medical studies can be found in Medline at the National Institute of Health National Library of Medicine.

"In the last decade 50% of U.S. pregnancies resulted in birth defects, neurological conditions such as ADD, dyslexia, autism, schizophrenia, other learning disabilities; mood disorders, eczema, other developmental disorders; or chronically unhealthy children," according to a recent report of the Na-tional Academy of Sciences (www.flcv.com/damspr4.html).

Peer-reviewed medical studies have documented that the majority of such conditions are caused "by exposure to toxic substances, with the most com-mon being the toxic metals: mercury, lead, arsenic, nickel, cadmium, cop-per, antimony, and aluminum. Pesticide, organochlorine, organophosphate, dioxin, polyaromatic hydrocarbons (PAH), and PCB exposures are also com-mon and can also cause such effects" (www.flcv.com/damspr4.html).

"Dental amalgam is the largest source of both inorganic and methyl mer-cury in most with several mercury amalgam fillings, and most with several fillings have mercury exposure levels 10 times that of the average person without amalgam" (www.flcv.com/damspr4.html). However, one cannot suppose that having mercury-filled teeth will lead to becoming a serial killer.

"Much of the developmental effects of mercury (and other toxic metals) are due to prenatal and neonatal exposures damage to the developing en-docrine (hormonal) system" (www.flcv.com/damspr4.html). It is common knowledge that any type of exposure to these toxic metals in vitro will create long-lasting effects for children and their futures.

"Prenatal and neonatal toxic metal exposure as well as chronic exposures to mercury, lead, arsenic, cadmium, nickel, and aluminum have been documented in medical publications and medical texts to cause common and widespread neurological and psychological effects including depression, anxiety, obsessive compulsive disorders, social deficits, other mood disorders, schizophrenia, anorexia, cognitive impairments, ADHD, autism, seizures, etc." (www.flcv.com/damspr4.html).

"Exposure to toxic metals causes ADHD, dyslexia, autism, and other neurological and immune conditions as a result of their neurotoxicity, immunotoxicity, and endocrine disrupting effects, as well as by causing deficiencies and imbalances in essential minerals and essential fatty acids; blocking essential enzymatic processes such as those necessary for digestion and processing of milk casein, wheat gluten, amino acids, vitamin B-6 and B-12; and causing 'leaky gut' and poor nutrient absorption. These enzymatic blockages and metabolic disorders prevent processing of necessary minerals and nutrients and result in neurotoxic metabolites in the body (www.flcv. com/damspr4.html).

"Metals toxicity and metabolic imbalances are major factors in behavioral disorders and problems of children—including violence, sociopathic behavior, juvenile delinquency, and criminality" (www.flcv.com/damspr4. html). The fact that there are direct correlations may help educators and child psychologists predict with certain accuracy when a child begins exhibiting psychopathetic behaviors that they may progress to serial killing as an adult.

"A hair element analysis of 28 recent mass murderers or serial killers found that all had patterns of metals toxicity and mineral imbalances typical of violent prone/sociopathic behavior" (www.flcv.com/damspr4.html). A 100 percent accuracy level would indicate that there is something to this toxicity creating and maintaining serial killer behaviors. If we can predict with this type of accuracy would it be a good idea to test all aggressive children? Could we save lives by a simple hair analysis? The answer seems yes, so why are we not doing it?

"Metals detoxification and nutritional treatment that deals with the essential mineral and essential fatty acid imbalances result in significant improvements in most of these conditions, including violent and sociopathic behavior" (www.flcv.com/damspr4.html). Identifying the possibility of solutions to preventing behavior and aggression problems is encouraging. It is key that children who are exhibiting behavioral and emotional acting out may need to be detoxified regularly as a means of good health practices.

"Common exposures in children have been documented for mercury (vaccines, mother's amalgam fillings, dental work, fish), lead (paint, soil, water fixtures, etc.), arsenic (treated wood, pesticides, shellfish, other foods, Scotchguard), aluminum (pans, processed food, medicines), cadmium (shell-fish, paint, piping), antimony (cosmetics), manganese (soy milk, welding, metal works)" (www.flcv.com/damspr4.html). All the common items listed above are part of many families' daily living. Are we inadvertently creating a generation of monsters?

The research studies quoted above bring a different perspective to some of the possible causes for why an individual may become a serial killer. It is necessary for scientists to continue their research in these factors and draw better correlations through more personal and historical review of past cases.

SOLUTIONS AND OPTIONS

So what can we do as educators, parents, social workers, and law enforcement officials? We can begin by recognizing the behavioral and emotional warning signs that are often exhibited early. We cannot ignore the troubled youth. We need to identify quickly and intervene early.

Since youths who become adult serial killers have a long phase of develop-ment we have the time to address the behaviors and give them the necessary skills. We have to empower them with positive coping skills, problem solving strategies and role models of positive human relationships and interactions. We have to intervene during childhood because once they reach puberty there is little to no hope left.

This population of at-risk youth who graduate to this level of dysfunction is very small. We can prevent the development of a serial killer. We need to aware and awake to the experiences that this youth has. We have to have the supports and the lines of communication need to be open so that the youth can reach out when they need to. They have to be able to get out of their heads and verbalize what they are feeling and thinking. They need to have an outlet to get help.

We have to be much more cognizant of the youth who withdraw into their own world. We need to keep them connected with the rest of the people in their lives. We cannot afford to allow them to plan their destruction. There has to be a better way. Our challenge is to find the right code for each one of these youths who becomes antisocial, conduct disordered, or oppositional so that we are able to give them much more functional skills that give them what they believe they need to be happy or successful.

We need to be aware that these young men can kill their entire family one moment and then go play baseball with their friends without one mo-ment of guilt or regret. We have to be aware that they lack the ability to be empathetic and to deal with them on a relationship basis is absolutely foolish and downright dangerous. They cannot form genuine relationships based on caring, sharing and honesty. Everything is black and white, it is all about accountability, you do this you get this, if you don't do this you don't get this. It is on a very primitive level.

In conclusion, if we stay alert we can prevent the monstrosities that they will commit. We can keep others safe and we can provide the help that this kind of youth is seeking, which is the ability to be connected in a positive way. Connectivity leads to relationships and therefore leads to a sense of value and purpose. All human beings deserve the right to be valued. The key is catching them early. Past eight years old it may be too late. ACT NOW!

4

Juvenile Prostitution, Child Trafficking, and Sex Tourism

The oldest profession is alive and well in the world. What is it about sexual activity that drives people to lose life, home, career, and sometimes freedom for the sake of an orgasm? Mankind is a funny animal that has attached all kinds of rules, expectations, and taboos around sexual fulfillment. In nature sex is for procreation and survival of the species. In humankind it is used not only for procreation but for manipulation, control, power, and intimacy.

It supposedly defines a connection of two beings in an altered way. It is meant to bring them closer together on another plateau. So why is sex partnered with violence and exploitation? Why is one's pleasure another's pain?

The prostitution of children, along with child pornography and child sex rings, involves the sexual exploitation of children for commercial gain. The number of children subjected to such exploitation in internationally renowned centers such as Colombo, Sri Lanka, Bangkok, Thailand, the Yaumati district in Hong Kong, the Philippines, India and Brazil, is not known. It is a very lucrative business with thousands of tourists flocking to these countries for more than just the historical sites.

The attractiveness to children and youth in their innocence has often been an aphrodisiac for some. They are incapable of functional adult relationships and therefore move toward a younger and at times more vulnerable partner. Often times these relationships are not consensual but based in some form of financial transaction or by fear of one's life.

Juveniles who enter the life of the streets often do so as a way to survive. Youths do not wake up one day and say I want strangers to use me sexually and abuse me. The movement to the streets often comes out of a need to escape an environment that may be detrimental or dangerous to the youth. The statistics are very varied as it is very hard to pin down the exact number of teenage prostitutes. Some have estimated from 300,000 to 600,000 youths at a time on any given day in the United States. The problem is that many of these youths are runaways and hard to track and some prostitute themselves while on the move and therefore cannot be accurately counted.

Sexual victimization is occurring in every state in the United States of America. There have been reports of children as young as eight years old being captured by the child welfare system. These children have been used and abused by a variety of adults. Many of these children become prisoners. They are sold on the streets and often end up with multiple sexual transmitted diseases, with HIV being one of the most common.

These children never have the opportunity to explore the regular milestones of being a teenager (going to prom, learning to drive a car, graduating from high school, going to college), instead their reality is they must go to work and be someone's sexual experience.

The youths are often victimized in many ways. They are bruised, tattooed, stabbed, and raped with regularity by both the pimps who control them and the clients. The youths accept this punishment and violence as a way of receiving affection from an adult or money from a trick.

A large number of juvenile runaways who are on the street and involved in prostitution also end up being recruited by pornography producers who make films with juveniles. Child pornography is a multibillion dollar industry. Many of the young street prostitutes have also been offered money to perform in amateur pornographic videos.

Child pornographers, like other sex offenders, seek victims in places where youths gather, such as shopping malls, fast-food establishments, and nonalcoholic clubs such as juice bars or under-21 clubs, and through unethical "modeling" agencies. The fact that juveniles are being recruited from the community, both for pornography and prostitution, is most disturbing and strengthens the resolve of the people who are outreach workers to make the youth "street smart," thus helping to ensure their right to a normal, healthy, corruption-free childhood. The result when many of these outreach workers try to get the youths off the streets is not always positive.

The pimps and pornographers will resort to violence to protect their investments and therefore these workers often become victims of personal violence and assaults. It is a dangerous job to get the youths off the streets.

What is child pornography? The law is quite clear at defining the parameters of the behaviors. "Under federal law (18 U.S.C. §2256), child pornography is defined as any visual depiction, including any photograph, film, video, picture, or computer or computer-generated image or picture, whether made or produced by electronic, mechanical, or other means, of sexually explicit conduct, where

- the production of the visual depiction involves the use of a minor engaging in sexually explicit conduct; or
- the visual depiction is a digital image, computer image, or computer-generated image that is, or is indistinguishable from, that of a minor engaging in sexually explicit conduct; or
- the visual depiction has been created, adapted, or modified to appear that an identifiable minor is engaging in sexually explicit conduct (www .missingkids.org).

Federal law (18 U.S.C. §1466A) also criminalizes knowingly producing, distributing, receiving, or possessing with intent to distribute, a visual depiction of any kind, including a drawing, cartoon, sculpture or painting, that

- depicts a minor engaging in sexually explicit conduct and is obscene, or
- depicts an image that is, or appears to be, of a minor engaging in graphic bestiality, sadistic or masochistic abuse, or sexual intercourse, including genital-genital, oral-genital, anal-genital, or oral-anal, whether between persons of the same or opposite sex and such depiction lacks serious literary, artistic, political, or scientific value (www.missingkids.com).

"Sexually explicit conduct is defined under federal law (18 U.S.C. §2256) as actual or simulated sexual intercourse (including genital-genital, oral-genital, anal-genital, or oral-anal, whether between persons of the same or opposite sex), bestiality, masturbation, sadistic or masochistic abuse, or lascivious exhibition of the genitals or pubic area of any person" (www .missingkids.org).

Child pornography is devastating to any youth who gets entangled in that world. The children and youth are often abused sexually until they either run away again or move on back to the streets as adult prostitutes. Either way the prognosis for these young people is very poor. Many of them will become victims of the underworld that they inhabit from an early time in their childhood. Frequently many of them will not see their adult years and will become a murder or suicide statistic.

Compared to adult prostitution juvenile prostitution is more likely to occur in large metropolitan cities. Juvenile prostitutes are more likely to work in groups and often will evade arrest. There are also gender differences between juvenile prostitutes. Male prostitutes tend to be older and will operate outdoors while female prostitutes are more likely to be younger and will operate in hotels or cars. Male prostitutes are more likely to be arrested by police than female prostitutes. The males are often more aggressive and may rob their tricks or even physically attack them if the encounter has turned bad. It does not matter how you study juvenile prostitution or from what angle you try to study it from, it is still the sexual exploitation of children.

A juvenile prostitute comes from all kinds of socioeconomic backgrounds and being poor is not the only factor that will decide if they engage in prostitution. They seem to all have in common chaotic, traumatic, and disorganized family lives. Because of this type of family dysfunction many of them do not have any type of vocational or functional skill, have very poor social skills, are unable to form healthy interpersonal relationships, and generally have a fear of intimacy because they are afraid of being rejected emotionally. It is better to not become involved and to remain dissociated from others and at times from reality.

There is a direct connection between juvenile prostitution and sexual abuse. The majority of juvenile prostitutes have experienced some level of physical, emotional, and sexual abuse. They have been victims of incest or forced sexual attacks leading to intercourse and physical trauma.

Sexual abuse seems to have the most negative and powerful impact on a child or youth. The age and time of development of child influence the ability to cope. "No single factor determines the psychological impact that sexual abuse has on the child. Rather, the intensity of the child's traumatization and the character of the psychological symptoms are influenced by several factors" (Bagley and King 1990).

The factors are:

- The child's stage of socio-sexual development, temperament, and understanding of the social sanctions against such behavior. Effects will thus depend on the meaning attached to it by the individual child.
- The nature of the abusive acts. Penetration, for example, will be more harmful than fondling or mere exhibitionism.
- The use of coercion and violence. Nonconsensual abuse appears to have a particularly harmful impact on the victim.
- The perpetrator's relationship with the child; abuse by a trusted caretaker leads to more intense emotional conflict for the victim.
- The perpetrator's proximity to the victim. Victims who cannot escape unwanted situations suffer more deleterious effects.
- The absence of familial support. The severely dysfunctional family not only increases the child's vulnerability to abuse, but causes excessive guilt through unsympathetic reactions and rejection of the victim.
- Intrusive negative effects of unwanted abuse are indubitably amplified when the abuse is accompanied by poor nurturance (as is the case with

many institutionalized abuse cases) and an unstable home life (Bagley and King 1990).

This list of factors may provide some form of awareness of the youth prostitute but it only touches the tip of the iceberg. Each child has a unique set of circumstances that come together for the youth to move toward becoming a prostitute.

Many of these youths do exhibit signs and symptoms prior to becoming prostitutes. "Children's reactions to the abuse are diverse and idiosyncratic" (Bagley and King 1990). Studies over the years have had mixed results and have not predicted with any level of accuracy the individual responses a youth or child will have to the abuse. "There is little doubt, however, that such premature exposure to sex gives rise to precocious sexuality, arrested psycho-sexual development and a distorted perception of love and affection" (Bagley and King 1990).

"Diminished inhibition, disrespect for personal boundaries, inappropriate sexual behaviors and excessive masturbation" were also reported with a level of consistency (Bagley and King 1990). They reported "increased levels of dissociation, accompanied by heightened aggressive and self-destructive behavior" that were common in children who had experienced some level of posttraumatic disorder after or during the abuse.

There is a difference in male and female sexual behaviors that often lead to prostitution. Males that are on the street as prostitutes do not identify as gay or even bisexual. They perform sexual acts for money and money only. Those that do identify as gay or bisexual are often a product of a broken home or of parents who have disowned them and they are forced to live on the streets. Because of their youthfulness, they are attractive and available.

Many male juvenile prostitutes have identified straight married men as their most valued customers. Many men now in their forties, fifties, and sixties were forced to marry to avoid detection of being gay, so in their later years they turn to young male prostitutes as an outlet for their desires and sexual actions.

Unfortunately, many young male prostitutes are forced to work the streets and often will engage in unprotected sex for cash. They are so in survival mode that the immediate gratification of cash overrides their good common sense. Many older males who use young males for prostitution are middle age men, often away from their families in a city far away from their home base, so that there is very little chance of being discovered. Many of these middle-aged men are married, businessmen, politicians, and/or men of position that cannot be out as gay men, but are secretly living their sexual life through prostitutes.

An interesting difference between male and female prostitutes is that males do not have a pimp. Many of them work as a solo agent. Some may have an older mature male as a sugar daddy but many are freelance. There are more and more agencies that take in young males and provide them with the safety of representing them through well-known rent-a-boy agencies; however very few are ever able to participate in these agencies because of their drug or alcohol dependencies or their mental health issues, which often leave them unreliable and unpredictable.

Many young juvenile prostitutes end up being HIV positive, drug addicts, or victims of assault and murder by individuals who are homophobic. Life on the street for such young males is often short and destructive and does not have a happy ending unless they meet someone who takes them in, and takes care of them, while providing them with the necessary skills to get out of the life and into a more productive career. The sad statistic is that many die way too soon.

TRAFFICKING OF CHILDREN

Trafficking in children is a worldwide problem affecting large numbers of children and youth in their prime of life. They are being harvested and kidnapped daily. "Some estimates have as many as 1.2 million children being trafficked every year. There is a demand for trafficked children as cheap labor or for sexual exploitation. Children and their families are often unaware of the dangers of trafficking, believing that better employment and lives lie in other countries" (www.unicef.org).

Trafficking of children can be a complex phenomenon. It involves a series of actions where children are moved from one location to another. These movements are not always illegal as there are times when parents have been lead to believe that their children are going on to better lives in another country. Illegality usually occurs whenever there are several movements of the child, leading to exploitation of the child. A child can be moved from one place legally and it becomes illegal once the child is passed on to another organization or group of traffickers.

Trafficking of children is increased by what are called push factors (poverty, family violence, family break-ups), where children and youth leave thinking that life has to be better in another town, city, state or country. On the other hand pull factors (economic differentials), create a community in need of new blood and new trade, especially if there is a high tourist demand for new youths. This increased need prompts certain traffickers to want to meet the need and become more financially wealthy for other initiatives.

Many of the children who have been seized are often unable to speak the language of the country they are in. They are badly treated, fed poorly, put in threatening situations and coerced into situations by fear of authority or by threat of violence. The youth then comply and become involved in the sex trade.

Child trafficking is a money making industry. It is usually very lucrative in that it fills the wallets of many criminal organizations. There are direct links with criminal activity and corruption. It is often hidden and hard to address. Trafficking in children takes away any hope that a child can live or have a regular family life and be in a safe environment. "Children who have been trafficked face a range of dangers, including violence and sexual abuse. Trafficked children are even arrested and detained as illegal aliens" (www. unicef.org).

Some facts:

- UNICEF estimates that 1,000 to 1,500 Guatemalan babies and children are trafficked each year, for adoption by couples in North America and Europe.
- Girls as young as thirteen (mainly from Asia and Eastern Europe) are trafficked as "mail-order brides." In most cases these girls and women are powerless and isolated and at great risk of violence.
- Large numbers of children are being trafficked in West and Central Africa, mainly for domestic work but also for sexual exploitation and to work in shops or on farms. Nearly 90 percent of these trafficked domestic workers are girls.
- Children from Togo, Mali, Burkina Faso and Ghana are trafficked to Nigeria, Ivory Coast, Cameroon and Gabon. Children are trafficked both in and out of Benin and Nigeria. Some children are sent as far away as the Middle East and Europe (www.unicef.org).

Trafficking comes in many different forms and has some very specific patterns of routes and behaviors. There are also different roles and responsibilities within the ranks of traffickers. Some adults are the ones who recruit; some transport, some deliver, some monitor and some clean up if there are problems with the youth. It is a very complex system of transfers and responsibilities, where some of the members only know the person directly in front and behind them in the process and have no idea about who is above them or behind. The organizational structure is built for the safety and protection of the traffickers.

The adults who are suppliers may be living in close proximity to many of the children and youth who are taken or apprehended. They often look for their victims by setting up a front in the form of modeling agencies, work services, employment placement centers, and even through ads in local newspapers for opportunities for youth. They do not apprehend or take the children; they merely identify and set the stage for others to remove the children. That way they maintain a certain level of decorum and safety in the community.

The second group of traffickers is those who are involved in the creating of false identification and documentation. They may work for government agencies, passport or licensing departments. These people then pass the child on to the movers, who begin moving the children through a series of individuals. Movers may be ferry drivers, boat captains, truck drivers and even individual drivers who carry the children from their town to the drop off point that has been pre-selected to exchange the child. At times what begins is a border-relay chain of drop off and pickups that are hard to follow or monitor, as they are often fluid and forever changing to avoid detection.

Finally, there are the receivers. These adults are the ones who receive the child or youth. They may be pimps, brothels, handlers who will begin to exploit the child for sexual commerce. The receivers are the ones who put the child to work in the sex trade. All along the route money is being made and exchanged with each stage of the child's journey. Trafficking is a very lucrative business. Big money is at stake and therefore the system is very sophisticated and complex and not easily cracked by government and law enforcement agencies. The only way trafficking will be slowed down is if there is international cooperation on the part of all governments.

Since 2001 the understanding of the nature of trafficking has improved and the complexities inherent in both the problem and responses to it are clarified. It is also clear that there are a number of unmet challenges that need to be addressed. Some of these are listed below by the Congress on Child Sexual Exploitation. The research initiated by the congress indicated that:

- There is still limited understanding of the complex links between poverty, gender, age, displacement, mobility, market factors, and HIV/AIDS, and how these lead to particular vulnerability to trafficking;
- Both government and civil society institutions as well as other stakeholders have still only begun to develop and implement effective interventions based on reliable research and evaluated according to appropriate criteria;
- The challenge of involving affected children and their families as active participants in initiatives addressing prevention, protection, reintegration and care is still largely unmet;
- There are few comprehensive regional and national rights-protective strategies to combat the trafficking of children;

- There are few models of recovery, repatriation, and reintegration actions that prioritize the interests and rights of children affected by trafficking;
- There is a clear need for models for institutional capacity building, measurement and evaluation, coordination, and strategic planning;
- The challenge of devising methodologies that provide evidence-based, comprehensive data on trafficking has not been met (www.csecworld congress.org).

In 2011 these gaps may lead, *inter alia*, to:

- Further victimization and criminalization of trafficking victims because of their illegal status;
- Skewed, inaccurate, and unsubstantiated statistics for the number of trafficking victims and the mechanisms involved, leading to inappropriate responses, wasted resources, and little or even negative impact;
- Draconian laws that, in an attempt to prevent trafficking, formulate penalties which are so stringent (death penalty and life imprisonment) that the conviction rate falls drastically due to imperfect investigation, weak evidentiary procedures, and reservations on the part of judges to mete out such harsh sentences;
- Further violations of the human rights of victims due to enhanced powers accorded to law enforcement agencies, many of whose members are corrupt and partners in the crime;
- Increased invisibility and inaccessibility of victims of trafficking when the wholesale and uncritical criminalization of the sectors into which they have been exploited (brothels and sweatshops, for example) encourages the criminals operating these sectors to move them underground (www.csesworldcongress.org).

Even though almost fifteen years have passed since the congress occurred in 1996 in Stockholm, Sweden, the problem still remains and seems to have grown at an amazing pace. This despite the fact that technology seems to be better at tracking the trafficking it is still occurring on a daily basis.

Trafficking has been identified as a fundamental human rights violation by both the United Nations Secretary General and the United Nations High Commissioner for Human Rights. Several significant international treaties and agreements have been promulgated to address the human rights violations involved in the trafficking of human beings, among them:

- Convention on the Elimination of Discrimination of Women (CEDAW) (1979)

- Convention on the Rights of the Child (CRC) (1989)
- Convention on the Protection of All Migrants and their Families (1990)
- The Hague Convention on the Protection of Children and Cooperation in Respect of Inter-country Adoption (1993)
- The Stockholm Declaration and Agenda of Action against Commercial Sexual Exploitation of Children (1996)
- The Rome Statute of the International Criminal Court (1998)
- International Labour Organization Convention No. 182 Concerning the Prohibition and Immediate Action for the Elimination of the Worst Forms of Child Labour (1999)
- The Optional Protocol to the CRC on the Sale of Children, Child Prostitution and Child Pornography (2000) (www.csecworldcongress.org 2001)

The international stage has been set and there are laws and conventions to end the issue of child trafficking and exploitation. The road is very complex and difficult to navigate. Many of the agencies collecting statistics are often not confident that they are truly representing the whole picture, but just a tip of a very big iceberg.

Often, people think that child trafficking is a problem of third-world countries but it is alive and well here in the United States. The United States has its own interstate domestic trafficking issues. The majority of the kids involved in this issue are runaways as young as twelve to thirteen who are scooped up and sold into prostitution. Many of the young girls are sold or pimped out to massage services, as escorts, child porn producers, private dancing clubs, recreational functions, photographers, and tourist destinations.

Many of these youths are handled by organized crime and are transported throughout the United States for functions and services. They are transported throughout the United States by a variety of means and using false identification in case of being arrested. The average age of the girls is twelve to fourteen, and eleven to thirteen for the boys and transgender youth. They are a commodity that brings a very high price to those who barter and sell within these ranks.

SEXUAL EXPLOITATION

Sexual activity is one that is often occurring behind closed doors and communities do not want to be in people's bedrooms, which may explain why so much exploitation of children occurs. These attitudes make children more vulnerable to sexual exploitation. "Myths, such as the belief that HIV/AIDS can be cured through sex with a virgin, along with technological advances such as the Internet which have facilitated child pornography and sex tourism targeting children, all add to their vulnerability" (www.unicef.org). People's stupidity and ignorance puts thousands of children at risk for exploitation every day somewhere in the world.

- Surveys indicate that 30 to 35 percent of all sex workers in the Mekong sub-region of Southeast Asia are between twelve and seventeen years of age.
- Mexico's social service agency reports that there are more than 16,000 children engaged in prostitution, with tourist destinations being among those areas with the highest number.
- In Lithuania, 20 to 50 percent of prostitutes are believed to be minors. Children as young as age eleven are known to work as prostitutes. Children from children's homes, some ten to twelve years old, have been used to make pornographic movies (www.unicef.org).

"Sex tourism involving children is defined as traveling to a foreign country with the intent to engage in sexual activity with a child. Under federal law (18 U.S.C. § 2423), it is illegal for a U.S. citizen to travel abroad intending to engage in sexual activity with a child younger than 18 that would be illegal if it occurred in the U.S. Individuals who commit these crimes are subject to prosecution in the U.S. even if the crime was committed on foreign soil" (www.missingkids.com).

Sex tourists come from all walks of life and can be international as well as local grown. There are two main types of child sex tourists; the situational and the preferential types, but a third and relatively unknown group is the sadistic sex tourists that operate underground and often undetected in a way. These sex tourists can be female, male, single, married, wealthy, or just your average individual. The interesting fact is that many sex tourists are not pedophiles or child sex abusers but individuals who take advantage of the situation when the child is offered for sexual activity.

The situational sex tourists are generally individuals for a variety of reasons, anonymity, being away from home and curious and social and moral constraints give themselves permission to take advantage and sexually act with these children. Many of these so called sex tourists will rationalize their activities in a number of ways. They may even say it is good for the child to have adult sexual relationships, or it is culturally acceptable to have sex with children in that particular culture, or even that it benefits the child's family and community. Whatever reasons these individuals use, the thinking is dysfunctional and abusive. No matter how you look at the behavior, it is still sexual exploitation of children in foreign countries.

The preferential child sex tourists want only children. They are relatively fewer in number than the situational sex tourists but can potentially harm many more children because of their ongoing desires for these children. There are several behavioral patterns that they engage in as a way to capture and abuse children. They are more likely to lure children with gifts, attention, and affection and may actually build some sort of trusting relationship with the child over time. They also will use threats, intimidation, and violence to keep the child from disclosing the sexual activity. They are all about keeping secrets and know what they are doing is wrong.

The preferential sex tourists that are predominately introverted do not have the ability to interact with these children on any other level. The primary purpose is sexual activity. They are also very poor communicators and are delayed socially and will target very young children for their sexual activity. They are unable to have satisfying sexual relationships with people of their own age group or social group. They are unable to communicate effectively with adults in a sexual or intimate fashion.

The last group is the sadistic sex tourist who is looking to inflict pain and exert control and power as part of the sexual encounter. This group often will resort to hurting and abducting, and may even kill, their victim during the sexual activity or period of capture. Their goals are often to use children for their pleasure and use pain as a way of achieving this pleasure.

These three types of sex tourist create a demand for children and because of that need there are many people who will gladly fulfill that need through an ongoing and ever changing supply of children.

The hot destinations of sexual exploitation for the tourist sex trade seem to be in South East Asia. Countries like Brazil and Thailand were at the forefront for many years and are still active but due to many efforts on the parts of the government and child protection agencies it seems to be decreasing. However, the areas of Vietnam, Cambodia, Ecuador, North and South Eastern Europe, Central America, and Indonesia are thriving as child sex tourism sites.

Child sex tourism is funded by hotels, airlines, and travel companies who create tours and opportunities for this type of tourism. The countries where the child sex tourism is occurring often will allow their guests to partake in these activities all for monetary gain and profit. Everyone wins except the child being exploited.

LIFELONG EFFECTS OF BEING EXPLOITED

Children who have been exploited for the sex industry end up with years of emotional and physical trauma. Many of them are unable to have positive human relationships. They are usually so scarred that they cannot hold on to employment, function in a normal setting such as a school, or be able to interact with same age peers. These children suffer from posttraumatic stress disorder, anxiety, and depression and often have attempted suicide. The correlation with being sexually abused and addiction is very high. Many have become drug addicts and are more prone to life-threatening diseases such as AIDS, hepatitis, malnutrition, and an early death.

Several organizations in the United States have attempted to reintegrate these children; however the success rate is very poor. The organization attempts to provide support, resources, and skills to enable the young adult to become self-reliant; however, the results are unsuccessful, as many just return to the streets as that is all they may have ever known. The goal is to prevent any of these children from ever entering the sex industry in the first place. Child trafficking for the sex industry must be terminated; otherwise many young lives will be sacrificed for the pleasure of those who profit and use these young people.

TRAFFICKING OF CHILD ORGANS

A relatively new concept that has now begun to surface is the trafficking of human child organs to wealthy countries. Recently headlines were made in Haiti after the devastating earthquake there in January of 2010, whereas certain medical personnel from the Israeli Defense Fund were extracting kidneys, corneas, and other organs for transport back to the Middle East.

Several children in Haiti had their organs extracted, specifically kidneys, and given to wealthy, ill children in the United States, Canada, Israel, and Western Europe. There is also a very large operation of organ trafficking from Mexico to critically ill children in the United States. There are reports of the Organ Mafia that operates along the Mexico-USA border that kidnaps Mexican babies for their organs and smuggles them across the border to clinics that remove the organs and sell them to parents of sick American children (www.atlzan.net).

There is an organization in Israel that is called the "Organ Mafia." It is a Zionist group that has been referred to as a fanatical cult. The FBI in their pursuit to stop trafficking in organs arrested nine rabbis between New York, New Jersey, and Zionist Israel. "The 'Rabbi Mafia' made tens of millions in human organs and laundered the money through phony Jewish charities and synagogues. Thirty-eight corrupt politicians controlled by the criminal Jewish rabbis were also arrested" (www.atlzan.net).

Israel has brought some 25,000 Ukrainian children into the occupied entity over the past two years in order to harvest their organs. This fact was brought to light because of a Ukrainian man's fruitless search for fifteen children who had been adopted in Israel. The children had clearly been taken by Israeli medical centers, where they were used for "spare parts" (www.atlzan.net).

The trafficking of children was brought to the world stage when the horrific killings of nineteen children and women occurred in the Indian slum of Nithari, close to the affluent area of Noida on the outskirts of India's capital in New Delhi (Gupta 2007). The world became aware of an industry that had been hidden in the shadows for many years. "There is huge demand and a market for body parts especially eyes, hearts and kidneys belonging to children. Estimates indicate that at least one million children have been kidnapped and killed in the past 20 years for organs" (Gupta 2007).

Gupta in his éxpose and newspaper article revealed that "the ongoing price for a kidney or eyes can fetch up to US $10,000 and a heart could cost US $50,000 or more." It has been estimated by several experts "that money laundering in this deadly trade accounts for up to 10% of the world's GDP, or as much US $5 trillion." As a result, the black market for children's organs is expanding and more and more children are kidnapped and killed (Gupta 2007). His research indicated that the majority of the victims that had been used in the trafficking of organs were primarily "from Asia, Eastern Europe, the former Soviet Union, Latin America and Africa." He cautioned his readers that trafficking also takes place in developed countries and not to have a false sense of security in thinking it cannot happen in your back yard here in America.

Those who take part in this trade make false promises about employment opportunities for the children and give money to the parents. Children are also stolen from orphanages, or handed over through a fake adoption process and killed for their organs. The intermediary may earn between US $50 and US $20,000 per child according to the source countries. In many cases, impoverished parents are sometimes persuaded to sell their children's organs for as little as US $500 (Gupta 2007).

The sadness in all of this is that everything has a price. Every part of the body from a child seems to be available for sale. People are desperate and will buy these organs as a way of saving their own family members no matter how or where the organ came from. Money is power. Life is cheap. There is such a huge demand for these organs that the demand oversteps the supply and therefore the price being paid continues to rise. There are reports of prices as high as $90,000 being paid for a live child who is transported to the United States for organ transplant.

There have been many advances in pharmacology, immune and rejection drugs that have made transplanting organs more of a routine procedure in the Western world. Human children have been reduced to a series of organs, blood, bones and are seen as a source of raw materials to be used by people who have the money to buy.

There are many horror stories of children kidnapped in one country and sold in another. The children in Latin America (Brazil, Uruguay, Mexico, Argentina, and Bolivia) are disappearing the fastest. They are often harvested by agencies who front the children up for adoption; however many never end up being adopted but are dissected for their organs instead. Countries like Pakistan are allowing the harvesting of children's organs and are therefore are inundated with Western tourists who are awaiting organs and are willing to pay large amounts of money for that particular needed organ.

This phenomenon has been around for many years; however it is receiving much more press as rings of child trafficking and organ trafficking are being unraveled and prosecuted. The business of child trafficking will not cease till the demand stops. Once people are able to understand that human life is valuable and that the child is a precious commodity and not some raw resource or organ bank, or object for sexual gratification that is for sale there will be no change in the behaviors and practices of the buyers.

In conclusion, this chapter was extremely difficult to write as it clearly showed the depths of depravity that humankind resorts to. Individuals on this planet will do whatever it takes to make a dollar. The lack of remorse, accountability, and human compassion is frightening. There are truly evil people in this world. These individuals need to be punished to the full extent of the law but also on a different dimension in another life. They need to be held accountable for their actions but also for all the misery they have caused to others. It is my hope that there is divine retribution somewhere.

5

Juvenile Court Justice System and the Laws

The juvenile criminal justice system came into existence because in the past if a youth or a child was involved in criminal activity he or she was turned over to their parents care and attention. It became clear early on that different parents took this responsibility in different degrees. It was also obvious that something needed to be done as parents were unable to control the activities of their children and youth. Instead, it became a responsibility of society.

Historically the juvenile justice system was created in the late 1800s to reform U.S. policies regarding youth offenders. Since that time, a number of reforms aimed at both protecting the "due process of law" rights of youth and creating an aversion toward jail among the young have made the juvenile justice system more comparable to the adult system, a shift from the original intent.

Back in 1824 the New York House of Refuge built a refuge to help youths who had been in trouble with the law. The purpose behind building this refuge was to provide rehabilitation not punishment. The juveniles were now housed in a juvenile reformatory setting rather than an adult prison. Beginning in 1899, individual states started to take notice of the effectiveness of having these juvenile reformatories and it became regular practice to build these refuges and provide care to these troubled youths.

The changes to the justice system were made as a way to protect young offenders. It was believed that it was their moral responsibility to make sure that young people received the right kind of guidance and support before they became adult criminals and were no longer salvageable. "The juvenile justice system exercised its authority within a *parenspatriae*' (state as parent or guardian) role" (www.lawyershop.com).

Each individual state now began to assume the responsibility of parenting these troubled young offenders until they began to exhibit positive changes, or became responsive citizens and adults. Youth were now treated as young offenders rather than adult criminals. Many of them were no longer incarcerated in adult prisons.

A new informal court designed for juveniles was created so as to be able to handle the youth offenders that were appearing in front of judges for the first time. Lawyers were generally not present and extenuating evidence, outside of the legal facts surrounding the crime or delinquent behavior, was taken into consideration by the judge. The process was founded on the fact that all youth could be reformed and saved.

The justice system was not formalized and did depend heavily on the interpretations of individual judges. Early reform houses were, in many ways, similar to orphanages. Many of the youth housed in the reformatories were orphans and homeless children that had been picked up as vagrants and were taken there without ever having committed a crime or an offense (www. lawyershop.com).

In 1967 a decision by the United States Supreme Court formalized the process of juvenile reform courts in that they had to begin to respect the due process of law rights of juveniles during their proceedings. It was no longer an informal process that depended on the whims of local judges but became a formalize series of steps. The ruling was the result of an evaluation of Arizona's decision to confine Gerald Francis Gault. Gault at the time was age fifteen and had been placed in detention for making an obscene call to a neighbor while under probation.

The Arizona juvenile court had decided to place him in the state industrial school until he became an adult (age twenty-one) or was "discharged by due process of law" (www.lawyershop.com). "The Supreme Court decision, delivered by Justice Abe Fortas, emphasized that youth had a right to receive fair treatment under the law and pointed out the following rights of minors:

- The right to receive notice of charges
- The right to obtain legal counsel
- The right to "confrontation and cross-examination"
- The "privilege against self-incrimination"
- The right to receive a "transcript of the proceedings," and
- The right to "appellate review" (www.lawyershop.com).

In 1968 Congress passed the Juvenile Delinquency Prevention and Control Act. The purpose of this act was designed "to encourage states to develop plans and programs that would work on a community level to discourage juvenile delinquency." It was a way to encourage states to become more responsible for their troubled youths.

The act would now make a financial commitment to helping the states pay for and manage youth offenders with federal funds. "The Juvenile Delinquency Prevention and Control Act was a precursor to the extensive Juvenile Justice and Delinquency Prevention Act that replaced it in 1974" (www.lawyershop.com).

JUVENILE JUSTICE AND DELINQUENCY PREVENTION ACT

The Juvenile Justice and Delinquency Prevention Act (JJDPA) of 1974 provides the major source of federal funding to improve states juvenile justice systems. The JJDPA was developed as a way to ensure that youth offenders or children should not have contact with adults in jails. Under the JJDPA and its subsequent reauthorizations, in order to receive federal funds, states are required to maintain these core protections for children:

The following are directly quoted from the law:

Deinstitutionalization of Status Offenders (DSO)

Status offenders may not be held in secure detention or confinement. There are, however, several exceptions to this rule, including allowing some status offenders to be detained for up to 24 hours. The DSO provision seeks to ensure that status offenders who have not committed criminal offenses are not held in secure juvenile facilities for extended periods of time, or in secure adult facilities for any length of time. These children, instead, should receive community-based services, such as day treatment or residential home treatment, counseling, mentoring, alternative education and job development support. (www.campaignforyouthjustice.org)

Adult Jail and Lock-up Removal

"Juveniles may not be detained in adult jails and lock-ups except for limited times before or after a court hearing (6 hours), in rural areas (24 hours plus weekends and holidays), or in unsafe travel conditions" (www.act4jj.org/about_requirements.html). This does not apply to habitual offenders or those convicted of a felony. This provision is designed to protect children from psychological abuse, physical assault and isolation.

"Children housed in adult jails and lock-ups have been found to be eight times more likely to commit suicide, five times more likely to be sexually assaulted, two times more likely to be assaulted by staff, and 50 percent more likely to be attacked with a weapon than children in juvenile facilities" (www. act4jj.org/about_requirements.html).

"Sight and Sound" Separation

> When children are placed in an adult jail or lock-up, as in exceptions listed above, "sight and sound" contact with adults is prohibited. This provision seeks to prevent children from psychological abuse and physical assault. Under "sight and sound," children cannot be housed next to adult cells, share dining halls, recreation areas or any other common spaces with adults, or be placed in any circumstances that could expose them to threats or abuse from adult offenders." (www.act4jj.org/about_requirements.html)

Disproportionate Minority Confinement (DMC)

States are now required to evaluate and monitor the disproportionate confinement of minority juveniles in all secure facilities and do ongoing report and progress monitoring as a way of making sure that there is not undue discrimination or negative selection of minority youth. Studies indicate that minority youth receive tougher sentences and are more likely to be incarcerated than nonminority youth for the same offenses. "With minority children making up one-third of the youth population but two-thirds of children in confinement, this provision requires states to gather information and assess the reason for disproportionate minority confinement" (Center for Children's Law and Policy).

In 2008 there was a reauthorization of the bill, which makes changes to the original bill in that it, among other things:

- eliminates the exception to detaining status offenders, the "Valid Court Order" (VCO) exception (a "loophole" added into the law in 1980);
- keeps kids out of adult jails and prisons (with limited exceptions);
- requires states to reduce racial and ethnic disparities;
- creates incentives for the use of programs that research has shown to work best; and
- refocuses attention on prevention programs intended to keep children from ever entering the juvenile or criminal justice systems (Thomas, Library of Congress).

The law clearly sets and defines guidelines for cities and government agencies to follow in the handling of their juvenile offenders. However, this legislation is still being discussed in the Congress even now in 2011. There is hope that it will be passed soon.

Educators, justice organizations, and local police agencies all know the law but the level of interpretation of this law seems to have a multitude of responses and enforcements. Can there be any type of consistency in any of these facilities? The goal of getting all centers to follow the same protocols in the USA, I believe is impossible. Later on in this chapter I will discuss the uniqueness of some of these centers and their philosophies around rehabilitation and programming.

"Juvenile courts handle an estimated 1.6 million delinquency cases and adjudicate youth delinquent in nearly 7 of every 10 cases each year." There is a very conservative estimate that approximately "200,000 youth have their cases processed in adult criminal court as a result of prosecutorial or judicial waiver, statutory exclusion for certain offense categories, or because they live in states with a lower age of criminal jurisdiction (age 16 or 17)" (www. act4jj.org/media/factsheets/factsheet_11.pdf). The juvenile justice system is overburdened with the demand and the lack of resources available to process and deal effectively with all these youth offenders.

"Of an estimated daily average of 97,000 incarcerated youth under 18, fully 25% of them are detained while awaiting placement or court proceedings. On any given day an estimated average of 7,000 youth under age 18 are inmates in adult jails and, of these, 90% are being held as adults" (www.act4jj.org/media/factsheets/factsheet_11.pdf). As one can see, the evidence is clearly articulated that there is a real need for juvenile justice reforms and action. These statistics continue to grow on a daily basis because of the amount of youth offenders who are taken off the streets due to a variety of felonies or petty crimes.

A large majority of youths who are confined are generally of a nonviolent nature and usually are highly amenable to rehabilitative services and supports. In 2011 the statistics indicate that there are about 2.2 million arrests of youths under age 18 each year. In nearly 50 percent of cases "the most serious charges are larceny-theft, simple assault, a substance abuse or liquor law violation or disorderly conduct. Juveniles who enter the justice system have been shown to suffer from higher than average mental health problems, learning disabilities and school failure, as well as under-addressed family intervention and support needs" (American Bar Association 2010).

The JJDPA, which was created in 1974 and most recently reauthorized in 2002, "provides for: a juvenile planning and advisory system spanning all states; federal funding for delinquency prevention programs and initiatives to improve state and local juvenile justice systems; operation of a federal agency (the Justice Department's Office of Juvenile Justice and Delinquency Prevention (OJJDP)) dedicated to training, technical assistance, model program development, as well as research and evaluation, to support state and local efforts" (www.act4jj.org/media/factsheets/factsheet_27.pdf). The mission of this organization is to have a consistent system on how to work effectively with juvenile justice.

Since 1981, "the JJDPA has been repeatedly reauthorized with bipartisan support based on the broad public consensus that children, youth and families involved with the juvenile and criminal justice systems should be safeguarded by federal standards for care and custody, while also upholding the interests of community safety and prevention of victimization" (American Bar Association 2010).

A youth has been arrested or collected by a police department, so what happens next. There is a well-documented legal route that must be followed to ensure that the youth's rights are maintained. How does a minor go through juvenile justice court?

The first encounter a youth has with the juvenile justice system is usually his or her arrest by a police department or an officer out on the street or on patrol. There are multiple entry points that troubled youth can enter the juvenile justice system. These may include "referrals" by parents and schools, delinquency victims, and probation officers who may have a single or multiple encounters with the youth. Once the youth has been assessed or evaluated by the arresting department, "a decision is usually made after arrest as to whether a youth should be detained and charged, released, or transferred into another youth welfare program" (www.lawyershop.com).

Once the officer handling the case has gathered a series of facts and evidence, often from personal interviews, makes a decision based on information obtained from the victims of the crime committed by the juvenile, the juvenile himself, the juvenile's parents, and any past records the youth has with the juvenile justice system, the decision to act or follow through on actual charges is made.

"Federal regulations require that juveniles being held in adult penitentiaries (while officials attempt to contact parents or make transfer arrangements) be kept out of 'sight and sound' of adult inmates, and be removed from the adult facility within six hours" (www.lawyershop.com). The procedure and protocols are quite clear: move them in and out rather quickly. The regulations in their wisdom try to protect these youths from possibly becoming victims in the local holding facilities.

Often times when a juvenile court case reaches the juvenile probation department, an intake officer will decide whether to dismiss it, handle it informally, or hear it formally (www.lawyershop.com). It is at this time that the receiving officer will make the decision as to what happens next. Lack of evidence will often result in the case being dropped. If the evidence is plentiful and the state has solid facts they will proceed in a formal way to begin charging the youth.

While a youth awaits trial he or she may be held in a "secure detention facility." "A judge will determine if the juvenile should be detained before and through the course of the trial, and define the intent of the detainment, in a 'detention hearing,' usually held within 24 hours of the arrest. A youth will typically be detained if he poses a threat to himself or public safety" (www. lawyershop.com).

INTAKE AND INVESTIGATION

A minor directed to a juvenile detention center must have their case evaluated in that the seriousness of the crime will direct the process of identifying the consequences. Depending on the charges the officer has a choice of what he or she can do. The probation officer can:

1. Release with a warning. The probation officer can give the minor a warning and let him or her go. This means the officer thought about what happened and decided to tell the minor where to get help instead of filing charges.
2. Informal supervision. The probation officer can put the minor on informal probation. The officer and the parents put conditions on what the minor can do. This can be: Going to school, taking part in community programs, having a better attitude, behaving better, having better relationships, not doing certain social things, or going to counseling. Informal probation usually lasts six months. After six months, if the minor did everything right, the probation ends. If not, the probation officer can file a petition on the original charge.
3. File charges. The probation officer can suggest to the DA's office to file charges. This is called filing a "petition" with the Court (www. scscourt.org/self_help/juvenile/jjustice/process.shtml).

Why Does the Minor Have to Stay at the Juvenile Center?

If a minor is found to not have committed a serious crime, then he goes immediately with his parents, a guardian, or a responsible relative, except if:

1. The minor doesn't have a parent, guardian, or responsible adult who can or will take care or control of him.
2. The minor doesn't have anywhere to live.
3. The minor can't support himself.
4. The minor's house isn't fit to live in, or if the minor is abused or neglected.

5. The minor has to be in custody to be protected, or to protect another person or property from the minor.
6. The minor will run away.
7. The minor broke a court order.
8. The minor is dangerous to the public (www.scscourt.org/self_help/ juvenile/jjustice/process.shtml).

In many cases where the probation officer decides to pursue the case and it will go to the district attorney, the adults that are responsible for the youth have to sign a promise to go to court and follow any conditions for release. There can be stipulated a variety of conditions before the youth is released. This may include letting the probation officer visit, search the minor's home and bedroom and take things as evidence in the case.

There are rules if a minor is to remain in custody. "The minor can't stay locked up more than 48 hours. Weekends and holidays do not count toward this 48 hour limit. But, a minor can stay locked up for longer if the DA files a petition or files charges in adult criminal court" (www.scscourt.org/self_help/ juvenile/jjustice/process.shtml).

What is a Petition?

A petition is a paper that provides:

> The name, age and address of the minor, what parts of the code sections the minor broke, if the charges are misdemeanors or felonies. The names and address of the parents or guardians, A short statement that says what happened, and if the minor is in custody or has been released. If the minor is locked up for a felony, the DA has to file the petition in 48 hours. If the minor is locked up for a misdemeanor, the DA has 72 hours to file the petition. There are no deadlines to file if the minor isn't locked up (www.scscourt.org/self_help/juvenile/ jjustice/process.shtml).

What is a Detention Hearing?

A detention hearing is held to decide if the minor should be taken out of their house or locked up in juvenile detention. If the minor is in custody there must be a hearing the day after the DA files the petition. The court usually explains the process, why they are locked up, what can happen in juvenile justice court and that they have the right to have a lawyer. If the minor doesn't have a lawyer, the court will assign one. If the court is informed that the parents can pay for a lawyer, the parents have to pay the county back; if the youth or family cannot pay then the state will cover the costs.

The minor can question the reasons they have been incarcerated. The minor has the right to question the process and witness and anyone who has provided evidence. The minor is able to call upon witnesses and present evidence of their own. But, for this hearing only, the court must believe that the petition is true.

The court needs to decide where the best placement is for the youth. This can mean that the minor is put on home supervision or in the juvenile center; those are basically the two choices. If a youth has been mandated to home supervision then monitoring occurs there. However, the court may take a minor out of their house because: "The minor didn't obey a court order. The minor ran away from a detention center. The minor would run away if the Court let them go" (www.scscourt.org/self_help/juvenile/jjustice/process. shtml). There is too much of a risk to allow them out on the streets or back into their home or community.

The minor needs protection because: "Their home isn't safe, The minor is or may become addicted to drugs, The minor has mental or physical problems, or What the minor did, called the offense is something they get locked up for. The Court needs to protect another person or property. A minor or the minor's lawyer can ask for a new hearing called a rehearing. They can have a rehearing if they ask to show the Court new evidence about why they should not be locked up" (www.scscourt.org/self_help/juvenile/jjustice/process .shtml).

What is a Jurisdiction Hearing?

The law and protection of youths' rights states that there must be a jurisdiction hearing on the charges within fifteen court days after the detention hearing if the minor is locked up. If the minor isn't locked up, the hearing must happen within thirty calendar days. The court can ask for a continuance if it believes that more time or additional evidence is required. Generally these continuances do not happen often as the court does not want to waste time and would like the issue dealt with as early as possible.

At the jurisdictional hearing the judge reads the petition and explains what it says in a way or language that a regular citizen can comprehend. The judge informs the parents or guardians that they may have to pay for fines or restitution if the minor is ordered to pay. It is at this time that the judge may ask the youth whether they actually did the offense of which they are accused of having done.

The minor can decide to enter a plea of guilty or not guilty. The judge must decide if the minor has a full comprehension of the situation and the consequences. If the minor states that the charges are false they can begin the process to prove it. It is at this time like in the detention hearing, the DA shows the court all of the evidence that has been gathered that supports their case and the reasons why they believe the youth is actually guilty.

The minor's lawyer plan of action may involve the following: Cross-examine the witnesses, object to evidence, present witnesses and evidence, and argue the case to the court. The youth is not required to testify. The judge alone decides if the allegations are true based on the evidence presented. There are no juries in juvenile justice court. If the judge decides that the petition is true, the court sets a hearing to decide how to care for, treat and guide the minor. If the judge decides the charges aren't true, the judge will dismiss the petition (www.scscourt.org/self_help/juvenile/jjustice/process.shtml).

What is a Disposition Hearing?

If a minor is found guilty by the judge then there is a hearing which is set right after the jurisdiction hearing. This hearing must be set within ten days if the minor is locked up, or thirty days after the DA filed the petition. At times these times may vary based on the circumstances and the parties involved which may ask for additional time.

At the disposition hearing, the judge decides what to do for the minor's care, treatment and guidance, including their punishment. As part of the preparation for the youth's hearing the probation officer has to write a "social study" of the minor for the court. This is then shared with all interested parties including the minor.

This social study includes all the relevant information that needs to be known so as to provide the best interventions or placement decisions. This study may include family and school history, past criminal history, a statement from the victim if the current charges are felonies, and recommendations. At the hearing, the minor or the district attorney can also provide additional evidence.

The victim is also allowed to provide the court a written or oral statement at the hearing. These judges need to take into consideration: How to protect the community and keep it safe, how to fix the victim's injury, and what's best for the minor when making their final decisions. The decisions are based on a variety of factors and are often influenced by individual differences and past history of involvement in the juvenile justice system.

The court can decide to follow a variety of steps: Set aside what the court decided (the "findings") in the jurisdiction hearing and dismiss the case. The judge believes for the interest of justice and the good of the minor or if the minor doesn't need treatment or rehabilitation that dismissing the case would be the best solution. The judge can put the minor on informal or formal probation with the probation department for six months where there is a more formalized evaluation or monitoring system to make sure the youth is complying with the rules or conditions in the decision.

The judge can also make the minor a ward of the court which takes away the rights of parents or guardians to make any type of decisions on the part of the youth. The court makes all daily decisions about the care, treatment and guidance for the minor without any input from parents or guardians. The judge can take full or partial control over a minor and the parents and/or guardians will have no influence or input. If the minor is a ward of the court, the judge can order different things. The list below starts with the less serious orders:

• Send the minor home on probation with supervision
• Send the minor to live with a relative
• Put the minor in foster care, a group home or institution
• Send the minor to a local detention facility, ranch, or county boot camp
• Send the minor to the division of juvenile justice (www.scscourt.org/ self_help/juvenile/jjustice/process.shtml).

If the minor is taken out of their home and put in a relative's home, in foster care, or a group home a case management plan for the future must be articulated and defined so all are aware of the conditions.

If the minor is locked up in a secured facility, the judge has to decide the maximum amount of time the minor can be locked up. If the minor goes to the division of juvenile justice, then the judge is very concerned about the youth and their criminal activities. This means jail time and that is decided by the type of offense and past history of the youth and their venture into the law arenas.

The judge can set terms and conditions for a minor on probation. The judge can order the minor to:

• Go to school without missing a day
• Go to counseling with the parents or guardians
• Stick to a curfew
• Follow every law
• Be tested for drugs and alcohol
• Do community service
• Go to a work program without pay
• Not see certain people
• Not drive. Or limit when and where they can drive
• Pay restitution to the victim. Or pay a fine

- Be searched without a warrant
- When a minor has to pay restitution or a fine, the parents or the person who has custody of the minor has to pay the restitution and fine (www. scscourt.org/self_help/juvenile/jjustice/process.shtml).

What Happens after the Disposition Hearing?

There are other things that can happen after the case is over.

Appeal: If the minor and/or family do not like the decision made by the judge then the appeal process begins where the lawyer has to file a notice of appeal. There is a sixty-day time limit to do this after the disposition hearing or after the judge made the order. The district attorney also has a right to appeal but rarely does as this means additional court and lawyer fees that may need to be covered by the state.

Ask to set aside the court order: The minor can ask the court to change or cancel a court order because of new evidence.

More restrictive disposition: If the minor isn't doing what they're supposed to do, they may have to go back to court to get a stricter sentence.

Ask to seal the minor's records: If, after five years there have been no other situations or crimes where the youth has appeared in juvenile justice court, he or she can ask for their records to be sealed if their only contact was with a probation officer. Once a youth turns eighteen and their case or the original hearing was in front of a judge, they can ask for their records to be sealed. The minor or a probation officer can ask the court to seal arrest records, the court file, probation records, and records of any other agency that may have records concerning a case.

The minor has to fill out an application to ask to have the records sealed and pay a fee. The probation department decides on the request.

A probation officer decides if the person can petition the court, fills out and files the petition, makes a report for the court, gets a court date, and tells the DA's office. The judge reads the petition and the report and makes a decision. The judge begins to look at the evidence and will evaluate what the minor did, if the minor finished their sentence and is rehabilitated, and if there are any lawsuits still in the courts about the incident. If the youth had a successful experience and stayed out of trouble then the petition to seal the records will be granted.

How Is Juvenile Justice Court Different from Adult Criminal Court?

Many educators and parents do not have a clear understanding as to what are the differences between juvenile justice court proceedings and adult criminal court proceedings. When a juvenile enters the justice system it is to decide if the charges in the petition are true and that there is sufficient evidence to proceed further in the process. The juvenile justice court is interested in finding out what is best for the minor and hold them responsible and attempt rehabilitation if possible based on the individual juvenile's issues. In comparison, the adult court finds people innocent or guilty and punish accordingly.

In the juvenile system there is usually a petition that is created that initiates the proceedings while in the adult system there is usually some complaint, investigation or a police report.

The first hearing for juveniles occurs once the juvenile has been locked up or put in some type of detention or if there is a jurisdiction hearing for a juvenile who is not locked up and may be in protective custody of parents. In adult court there is an arraignment of the defendant to figure out if there will be a trial.

In the juvenile justice system there is no bail offered. In the adult system bail can be an option based on the offense or crime. This amount varies based on the flight risk of the adult. This is often set by the individual judge on the recommendation of the district attorney.

In the juvenile justice system there is very little or no plea bargaining while in the adult system this is a core component in many cases. Adults can negotiate reduced charges or sentences based on a variety of factors.

In the area of fact finding adults require a trial where evidence is uncovered while all the facts about the juvenile case are done within a jurisdiction hearing. Adults have the right to ask for a jury trial while juveniles who remain in the juvenile system do not have access to trial by jury.

Both adult and juvenile offenders have a right to appointed counsel if they are not able to pay for one or the parents of the juvenile won't pay for any of the defense costs. It is often the case that juveniles do not have the financial means to pay for lawyers or representation and these costs are absorbed by the state.

In the area of judgments adults are either guilty or innocent. While in the juvenile justice system the judge sustains or doesn't sustain the petition which means that he or she believes the petition presented to be true or not. The judge takes action based on the belief of the facts within this petition.

Adults once convicted receive a sentence while the juvenile receives a disposition. Adults often go to jail to do their time and do not often get rehabilitation services. Juveniles are in a detention center where hopefully they have access to resources for rehabilitation and possibility of further education. If the process has taken an extended period of time adults receive credit for time while awaiting trial while the juveniles do not. The juveniles begin their time once the disposition is complete (www.scscourt.org/self_help/juvenile/jjustice/process.shtml).

WHEN ARE MINORS TREATED AS ADULTS?

There are two times when a youth will bypass the juvenile justice system and go directly to adult court and be tried as an adult with the adult criminal justice procedures and processes.

Direct Filing

In 2000, there was a major change in how states dealt with youth offenders. After intake and screening, the case is forwarded to the district attorney who can choose to file charges in adult criminal court directly. The district attorney evaluating the case takes into account whether the youth:

- "Is already a ward of the Court for a different felony crime, was 14 or older when the crime happened and has a record."
- "Was at least 16, but under 18, when the new crime happened."
- "Is charged with: 1st degree murder, attempted, premeditated murder, aggravated kidnapping if the penalty is life in prison, serious felonies when the minor fired a weapon and some sex crimes using force" (www .scscourt.org/self_help/juvenile/jjustice/process.shtml).

If the DA files the case in adult criminal court, the minor is treated like an adult with the same rights and must follow the same procedures. This means that the minor can have the same sentence as an adult if they're convicted of the same crime. It is at the judge's discretion whether the minor should get a juvenile disposition as recourse to an alternative consequence.

Fitness Hearing

After the detention hearing and before the jurisdiction hearing, the DA can ask for a hearing to decide if the minor should be in juvenile justice court. The only reason that this may occur is that the youth is extremely dangerous or the crime committed is a felony. The probation officer at this time would present the social study and other evidence needed to speak on the behalf of the youth or the district attorney.

The judge looks at this to decide if the minor would do well with the care, treatment, and programs in the juvenile justice program or should go directly into the adult prison system.

At the hearing, the judge looks at the probation report and all supporting evidence and makes a decision. The court looks at the following factors when contemplating the path or direction of the consequences: It will look at "how sophisticated the crime was, if the minor can be rehabilitated (learn to improve), the minor's criminal history, what happened before when the minor tried to improve (rehabilitation), what happened this time and how serious the charges are" (www.scscourt.org/self_help/juvenile/jjustice/process.shtml).

If the judge decides that the minor should stay in juvenile justice court, they'll have a jurisdictional hearing; if not, the court dismisses the petition and sends the minor to adult criminal court.

The district attorney files a complaint to start the case in adult criminal court. The minor has to deal with all the laws and procedures and has the same rights as an adult and unfortunately the same punishments as an adult who has committed the same crime.

There is no appeal from a fitness hearing generally. If you want the court of appeals to evaluate a decision a writ must be presented and written objecting to the judge's decision. To get a writ, the minor has to file an application for a writ to the court of appeals. One only has twenty days to do this after the minor's first court date in adult criminal court.

Community Release

If the minor is released to this program, he or she will be strictly supervised. A counselor is involved in all aspects of the minor's life and will have daily check in with the minor's school, boss and parents and the minor themselves. The counselor is responsible for writing the progress reports with the ongoing supervision. In some cases, the minor will be electronically monitored. At the disposition hearing, the judge will decide if electronic monitoring will be part of the minor's probation conditions.

A program that has had success in working with juvenile offenders is called FOCUS. This acronym stands for "First Offender Close up Services." This special program deals with minors who are at risk because of:

• Their age,
• Doing badly in school,
• Family problems,
• Drug abuse, or
• Breaking the law.

These factors have been identified as putting a youth in danger of becoming a repeat offender. The court will often send this type of youth to the FOCUS program, to look at the minor and the minor's family and generate what they hope to be a successful intervention. A team of people meets every week to talk about how the minor is doing and what the minor and the family needs. A probation officer from the FOCUS program will supervise the minor closely until probation ends. That way there is some consistency in the program that enables the youth to be monitored and hopefully successful.

Electronic Monitoring Program (EMP)

A youth can be forced to wear an electronic monitoring device instead of being sent to juvenile hall. The tagging can occur at any time during the procedures. Youth wearing these devices are supervised by a probation group counselor. There are two ways that the monitoring can occur: firstly through voice recognition or secondly a transmitter attached to the ankle. Voice recognition is when the probation department calls the minor's house at random. The minor talks into the phone. Computer matches the voice to a recording of the minor's voice and identifies the youth in question. If the voice does not match then an alarm does sound and a site visit may occur.

If the minor has a transmitter attached to the ankle, the probation department calls a monitoring device in the minor's house. If the minor left without permission or disconnected the equipment, it sets off an alarm and a probation officer may seek out the juvenile.

Alternative Placement Academy (APA)

APA's goal is to give minors who break the law an alternative to being locked up or put in a group home. If the minor qualifies, they can be put in a co-ed school for grades nine to twelve. The minor:

- Has eight hours of school or job training a day
- Has a lot of supervision
- Gets wrap-around services
- Gets electronic monitoring
- Gets drug testing
- Has to pay restitution (compensation) to the victim
- Goes through a family strengthening program, and
- Has to take responsibility for their actions (www.scscourt.org).

Evening Reporting Center (ERC)

The Evening Reporting Center in California is an alternative to juvenile hall. It began operations in 2006. The ERC offers a thirty-day program that operates from three to nine p.m.; the program is extremely structured and defined so that young people get the chance to get help in a supportive, "family-like" environment. The youth who generally are excellent candidates for this program are those youths who have violated probation, or have committed minor crimes such as petty theft or drug use. They get help with all kinds of issues that are putting them in danger of failing in society and failing on probation. The hope is to prevent failure and becoming a chronic offender or liability on the juvenile justice systems (www.scscourt.org).

COURT AND LEGISLATIVE DECISIONS

The following are some court and legislative decisions that have affected the juvenile justice system.

CARE Act: "The CARE Act was brought before the Senate in 2003. The act is designed to allow tax deductions for individuals who make charitable contributions. The aim of the program is to promote giving to community programs that benefit youth and their families. Such positive activities lower youth crime" (www.lawyershop.com).

The Violent and Repeat Juvenile Offender Accountability and Rehabilitation Act: In 1999, Congress enacted the "Violent and Repeat Juvenile Offender Accountability and Rehabilitation Act." The act increased punishments for juvenile violent offenders based on its assessment that, "the rehabilitative model of sentencing for juveniles, which Congress rejected for adult offenders when Congress enacted the Sentencing Reform Act of 1984, is inadequate and inappropriate for dealing with many violent and repeat juvenile offenders." The legislation requires violent juveniles to take responsibility for their actions. One of the most controversial aspects of the act is that it allows youth accused of violent crimes to be federally prosecuted as adults at the age of fourteen. The bill also tightens gun control laws (www.lawyershop.com).

In re Gault: The *In re Gault* decision of 1967 ensured that youth would be entitled to certain due process rights. Subsequent changes in the formality of the juvenile court made hearings less like civil proceedings and more like criminal trials. The rights juveniles were guaranteed in 1967 were the right to receive notice of charges, the right to obtain legal counsel, the right to call witnesses, the right against self-incrimination, the right to appeal a decision, and the right to receive a transcript of court proceedings (www.lawyershop.com).

In the last twenty years there have been all kinds of programs and laws that have tried to control the use of guns, violence in the schools and communities and the acting out of children and youth. The numbers have been steadily growing with less and less success. The juvenile justice system has been researched consistently yet there are very few successes. There does not seem to be a magic pill or solution. The juvenile justice system is failing, it is faced with the discouraging prevalence of crime, a lack of funding for preventative

programs, and disagreement over the principles that define its very foundation. The lawmakers do not seem to be able to get on the same page when it
comes to juvenile offenders.

America is and has been struggling with the following questions about
juvenile justice for years. At the present there are only questions and very
few directive answers. The following questions have motivated researchers,
scientists, and lawmakers to find answers that may solve many of the issues
in the juvenile justice system.

- At what age is a juvenile to be held accountable for his or her actions?
- Is it permissible to try and punish minor offenders as adults?
- Can the death penalty be applied to juveniles?
- To what extent is a parent or guardian responsible for the actions of a
  youth in his or her care?
- Why do minority youth make up such a disproportionately large portion
  of prison inmates?
- Is it appropriate that parents who can afford to independently fund reha-
  bilitation for their children may care for them at home, when otherwise
  they would be placed under the care of the state?
- Are juvenile and adult penitentiaries unsafe places for youth to live?
- Is the incarceration of juveniles counterproductive?
- Do juveniles have an increased right to confidentiality? (www.lawyershop
  .com).

As an educator in the field for over thirty years I have had the opportunity
to see every type of student, child, and disorder. I have been given the chance
to see all kinds of behaviors in all kinds of situations. I would like to respond
individually with the questions listed above by the juvenile justice system.

At what age is a juvenile to be held accountable for his or her actions?
All people regardless of age should be made accountable for their behaviors;
the point to remember is whether or not the youth has the skills, knowledge,
cognitive ability, and guidance to know the difference between what is right
or wrong. Once that determination has been completed the adults responsible
need to develop a plan to teach not punish. Only with appropriate teaching
can a youth learn new behaviors.

Is it permissible to try and punish minor offenders as adults? In this situation
one must refer to what was mentioned above. Does the youth have the necessary skills or cognitive ability to make choices? A youth's physical years does
not ensure the capacity to understand the ramifications of one's action. There
is no magic number—fourteen or fifteen or sixteen—when a youth suddenly
becomes able to process choices as an adult. Brain research indicates that the

brain is still forming up to age twenty-five. Youths do not become effective problem solvers till around that age, so should youth offenders be treated differently up to the age of twenty-five? Something to consider!

Can the death penalty be applied to juveniles? The death penalty in my opinion is never justified in any case when it comes to juveniles. They do not possess the necessary life experience or cognitive ability to truly understand all of their actions. An eye for an eye is a barbaric practice that humankind needs to abandon as something from a time of less enlightenment. It does not stop future violence or deter juveniles from committing crimes. Fear of loss of life very rarely factors into the juvenile committing the crime. The crime is often impulsive, random or poorly planned in the majority of cases.

To what extent is a parent or guardian responsible for the actions of a youth in his or her care? There needs to be some shared responsibility; however some juveniles are uncontrollable from an early age and come from truly functional families. There is evidence of genetic studies that have indicated a correlation with a predisposition to violence as far back as several generations.

The accountability for parents needs to be evaluated on a case by case basis and must take into consideration the ability of the parents as well to be able to control their children but also their capacity to be parents. A dysfunctional adult will often create a dysfunctional juvenile; at what point do you break the cycle and change the life pattern of this family? In an ideal world parents would be made accountable but in many cases the parents are as lost as their children.

Why do minority youth make up such a disproportionately large portion of prison inmates? This is a cultural question. One needs to look at how ethnic groups are served in our society and in our schools. Oftentimes the service is poor and not equitable. These populations do not have access to great schools and communities because of socioeconomic issues such as poverty and exposure to crime and chaotic communities.

The American dream of liberty, equality, and justice for all is truly not available to all. As long as this division occurs in American society so will disenfranchised and disillusioned youth exist. They are seeking what they think will make them happy and good American citizens. Unfortunately the American dream will never be a reality for these juveniles.

Is it appropriate that parents who can afford to independently fund rehabilitation for their children may care for them at home, when otherwise they would be placed under the care of the state? Services and facilities are overburdened by the need due to sheer numbers. If families can help support and fund this process then there needs to be collaboration between all parties to ensure that the goal is rehabilitation and that the youth can become a productive member of their community.

Just because one has the financial resources does not mean they will be able to provide effective interventions that will lead to change on the part of the juvenile. The choice of placement needs to be evaluated carefully and chosen based on the ability to effectively change behavior in the long run and not be a short-sighted short-term solution.

Are juvenile and adult penitentiaries unsafe places for youth to live? Absolutely, one only needs to look at the statistics of the assaults, murders and outrageous behaviors that exist within the walls of these institutions. They are one of the most regulated institutions but have the highest number of victims and acts of violence. It does not take a genius to figure out that by putting a combination of criminals in one place that it becomes a replica of the hierarchy of society.

The strong and powerful will control the weak and young. There is enough research to indicate that juveniles in adult prisons are at risk of sexual and physical attack and death. The mixing of the two groups succeeds in making sure that the juvenile will come out worse than he was prior to going in or will be carried out in a casket. The nature of man is to survive and the domination of the strongest will ensure survival, so prison is no different, only the strong will live for another day, the weak will die. The principles of natural selection in nature have been proven accurate once again.

Is the incarceration of juveniles counterproductive? For some yes, for others it is absolutely necessary to protect society. This is a case-by-case decision. The juvenile who runs away and commits petty crimes needs to be given education, skills and a promising future instead of jail. The juvenile who is mentally ill and commits a crime needs mental health services and care to navigate the mental illness, not jail.

The juvenile who is pathological needs to be incarcerated for their protection but most of all for those who may become their victims. A clear and concise evaluation of each individual's needs must be comprehensive so as to best serve the juvenile and society. Professionals who work with juveniles need to be excellent evaluators and intuitive in their handling of all their young charges. Accurate assessment is the key to success.

Do juveniles have an increased right to confidentiality? Confidentiality is a right that we all should have. Does keeping secrets protect or influence the juvenile's likelihood of being able to begin over? One must take into account whether there is a safety risk. If the juvenile is being an impulsive teenager or has engaged in stupid behaviors and that being kept confidential allows the youth to do restitution and never repeat the behavior, then yes, they should be given a second chance and their incident kept confidential.

If a juvenile has a long history of violence and crimes against people, then no, his or her right to confidentially should not be kept if other people are at risk if they are unaware of this potential or predisposition toward violence. Records should be assessed and integrated into police and justice systems so that there is ability on the part of law enforcement officials to track and make connections when doing investigations.

At times these confidential records have information that may have prevented a future crime. Instead of being reactive, law enforcement agencies can be proactive in being able to monitor juveniles so as to prevent an incident, not show up once the crime or violence has become another statistic.

Through research into which programs have been effective—both at home and abroad—policy makers hope to develop strategies that will decrease crime rates in future years. By taking the initiative to build anti-crime programs structured to fit local needs, community leaders have generated a plethora of information on which programs work, where they work, and what it takes to carry them out. Current U.S. policy aims to balance public safety with the effective rehabilitation of youth, and courts seek to individualize recommendations to fit the situations of young offenders.

It seems that lawmakers are active in trying to change the culture of youth violence by enacting laws and processes that will hopefully rehabilitate and redirect troubled youth. Transforming troubled lives is never easy. The important factor in this discussion is that community members, educators, politicians and justice officials are all invested in making things different and hopefully better for all.

6

Juvenile Detention Centers

Detention of juveniles in New York City began shortly after the opening of the New York State penitentiary in 1797. Prior to that time, as juvenile crimes were rare, the state preferred to allow parents to deal with the misbehavior of their children—a practice rooted in English common law. Parental authority was the accepted first tenant of youth treatment, and the state was hesitant to assume the failing parent's duties. Life has sure changed since that time. What has gone wrong?

Juvenile detention centers (JDCs) tend to be large holding tanks for a variety of children and youthful offenders. It seems that each one of the JDCs has specialized rules, procedures, and protocols. There does not seem to be any rhyme or reason as to why some facilities do what they do in terms of their programming. JDCs have a mandate to keep dangerous youth offenders off the streets and in protective custody. In 1974 an act was developed to help in the processing and handling of youth offenders.

The Juvenile Justice and Delinquency Prevention Act was created as a way to respond to the increasing number of youths coming into the system. It was revised in both 2008 and 2009; however, in April 2010 in Washington it failed to make the House of Representatives agenda and was not voted upon and therefore not reauthorized to the disappointment of many juvenile youth advocates.

The United States of America does not have one juvenile justice system, but rather fifty-one different sets of rules and procedures in handling troubled and offending youth. This fragmented system leads to misinformation, miscommunication and lack of consistency across state lines.

More than 100,000 teenagers are held in custody every day at costs ranging from $100 to more than $300 per day. Most of these youths are housed in large, congregate-care corrections facilities—detention centers for those awaiting court hearings and training schools for those who have been found delinquent.

Who is incarcerated? Few of these confined teens are serious offenders. Most are charged with nonviolent property or drug crimes. One third is confined for status offenses (such as running away and truancy), public order violations and technical violations of probation rules (like missing curfew). Approximately two-thirds are youths of color (Blueprint for Juvenile Justice Reform 2006).

Zero tolerance policies are one factor driving up rates of juvenile incarceration. First enacted into law by state legislatures and eventually by Congress in 1994, zero tolerance measures were aimed at dangerous students bringing guns to school. "Over the past decade, however, disciplinary policies mandating severe punishments—suspensions, expulsions and referral to law enforcement—have been expanded in many districts to cover a broad canvas of student behaviors, including not only possession of weapons, drugs and alcohol, but also prescription and over-the-counter medications and common objects like nail clippers as well as making threats, truancy, tardiness, and vague, catch-all categories like "insubordination" and "disrespect" (www .ytfg.org/documents/Platform_Juvenile_Justice.pdf).

Zero tolerance policies are often responsible for driving struggling students out of schools and into the juvenile justice system, dramatically increasing its racial disparities as so many of the struggling students are ethnic minorities. They are unable to be successful within a white-dominated public school system. Several jurisdictions across America, most notably in the larger urban cities, report that almost half of all their referrals to juvenile court originate from schools. It is a known fact that incarceration is less effective and more expensive than keeping kids in school (Blueprint for Juvenile Justice Reform 2006).

The placement of youth in secure detention facilities, which deprive both adjudicated and unadjudicated youth of their freedom, often conflicts with the historical justification that secure juvenile detention should only be used: "(1) to ensure that alleged delinquents appear in court and (2) to minimize the risk of serious reoffending while current charges are being adjudicated" (National Juvenile Detention Center).

Juveniles upon arrest are often placed in highly restricted detention centers while awaiting a hearing. This has not been an effective use of the facilities as the young offenders are housed in facilities designed to accommodate juveniles for only brief stays, youth find themselves detained for substantial periods during both the preadjudication phase and prior to implementation of the dispositional plan.

They become part of a population consisting of a mix of both adjudicated and unadjudicated youth as well as juveniles who committed status offenses and actual crimes and are often put at severe risk both physically and emotionally. Consequently, kids who have minor issues such as truancy may be housed with youths who have committed severe crimes of violence. This makes no sense whatsoever.

The problems with how detention is applied for juveniles with less serious offenses must take into consideration that involving defense attorneys in juvenile proceedings at an earlier stage and advocating for creative alternatives to secure detention would be a proactive step toward protecting youths but also using the facilities for what they were designed to do (National Juvenile Detention Center).

From one parent's perspective: "A child facing incarceration should have a right to know what his options are and how to access those options. Having a well-trained and caring legal advocate is critical. . . . Perhaps many parents think they know and understand what may lie ahead [but] we are mistaken. Our son and our family are still paying for that mistake" (Juvenile Justice Project of Louisiana).

There are no easy ways of getting recent statistics. The last census of juveniles in resident placements was done in 2006. Below you will read the findings of this census. As you can readily see, at the beginning almost 93,000 youths have been involved in some type of offense and are now housed in a residential youth center. It is my belief that the statistics have continued to grow and the crimes have continued to flourish. There are rumors of between 100,000 and 300,000 youths who are incarcerated in a juvenile detention center of some type.

DETAILED OFFENSE PROFILE FOR UNITED STATES, 2006

Because of the lack of recent data the information presented is an overview of the more common areas of concerns. The issue of delinquency is paramount and the numbers have surpassed ninety thousand. The most common offenses are simple assault, followed by aggravated assault, sexual assault, and robbery (Sickmund, Sladky, and Kang 2008). The crimes against persons account for the largest percentage of juvenile offenses.

Offenses against property are predominately burglary, theft, and auto theft. The reasons behind these offenses are that theft is the fastest access to acquiring quick money or possessions or a form of retaliation. Drug trafficking is relatively low as many of the youths do not get charged or detained for these offenses. Alcohol infractions are few and indicate that often law enforcement will not detain for alcohol possession or drunkenness (Sickmund, Sladky, and Kang 2008).

As part of the research in detention centers, there was a curiosity from the information cited above where the distribution was in terms of regions and states. Were there hot zones in this country that had many more than others? Were there any risk factors in the region or social-economic factors to explain the population in detention centers? There were no surprises, with California, Texas, Florida, and New York out in front in terms of their numbers. The states that surprised this researcher with their high numbers were Pennsylvania and Ohio (Sickmund, Sladky, and Kang 2008). One might begin to surmise that the harsh economic times these two states have had in the past few years are a possible explanation. When the data was divided by region, the Northeast was relatively low considering the amount of population present and the Southwest including California was quite high. Many of the southern states were low while several Midwest states were in the top ten (Sickmund, Sladky, and Kang 2008). It is now time to consider doing another census to get an accurate picture of what types of juvenile offenses are prevalent and where they are housed and hopefully rehabilitated.

Research demonstrates that children in adult institutions are five times as likely to be sexually assaulted, twice as likely to be beaten by staff, 50 percent more likely to be attacked with a weapon, and eight times as likely to commit suicide as children confined in juvenile facilities.

Case examples:

- In Ohio, six adult prisoners murdered a seventeen-year-old boy while he was incarcerated in the juvenile cellblock of an adult jail.
- In Florida, a seventeen-year-old mildly retarded boy who had pleaded guilty to sexual battery was strangled to death by his twenty-year-old cellmate. Both the youth's attorney and the sentencing judge had tried unsuccessfully to get the boy into treatment rather than prison.
- In Ironton, Ohio, a fifteen-year-old girl ran away from home overnight, then returned to her parents, but was put in the adult county jail by the juvenile court judge to teach her a lesson. On the fourth night of her confinement she was sexually assaulted by a deputy jailer. More than five hundred children had been incarcerated in the jail over a three-year period, many for truancy and other status offenses (which would not be crimes if committed by adults).
- In Boise, Idaho, a seventeen-year-old boy was held in the adult jail for failing to pay $73 in traffic fines. Over a fourteen-hour period, he was tortured and finally murdered by other prisoners in the cell. Another

teenager had been beaten unconscious by the same inmates several days earlier. More than 650 children had been held in the jail over a three-year period, 42 percent for traffic offenses and 17 percent for status offenses.

- In LaGrange, Kentucky, a fifteen-year-old boy was confined in the adult jail for refusing to obey his mother. Soon after he got in the jail, he took off his shirt, wrapped one sleeve around his neck and the other around the bars of his cell, and hanged himself. Jail records showed that 1,390 children were held over a four-year period, most for minor and status offenses.
- In rural Glenn County, California, a fifteen-year-old girl was taken to the local jail for staying out past curfew. After several days, she had a detention hearing, but was not released. When she went back to her cell, she hanged herself.
- In Knox County, Indiana, a seventeen-year-old girl was held in the county jail for shoplifting a $6 bottle of suntan lotion. Despite a history of emotional problems, she was put in an isolation cell. Several hours later, she committed suicide by hanging herself (Building Blocks for Youth Factsheet).

It is a proven fact that by putting juveniles in adult prisons you are creating a better criminal—one who is more likely to continue on the path of crime instead of rehabilitation and become a good upstanding citizen. Youths do not belong in adult prisons for any reason. As much as it may be desired by many, youths in adult prisons end up either dead or victimized or damaged for the rest of their lives. Those results are too high of a price to pay for some of the actions that youths are committed to adult prisons for.

Every year, hundreds of thousands of youths are placed in juvenile detention and corrections facilities and on any given day, more than 8,000 youths are held in adult jails. The Office of Juvenile Justice and Delinquency Prevention's national survey shows overcrowding in most of the juvenile facilities, making these dangerous and unhealthy places for youths. Youths in adult jails and prisons are in even more danger as they are at serious risk of abuse, assault, and suicide.

Crowding has an impact throughout a facility, making it difficult to provide adequate medical and mental health services, education, and recreation. Crowding also raises the tension level between youths and staff, and leads to increased use of isolation and restraints. A national survey of juvenile detention and corrections facilities, conducted by ABT Associates and published by the federal Office of Juvenile Justice and Delinquency Prevention, found that crowding is pervasive in these facilities: more than 75 percent of youths incarcerated nationwide are housed in detention and corrections facilities that violate standards relating to living space.

A significant number of youths in the juvenile justice system have mental health disorders. An estimated 50 to 75 percent of incarcerated youths nation-wide have a diagnosable mental health disorder. Current studies indicate that there is a lack of screening, assessment and treatment of children with men-tal health problems, and without appropriate treatment, youths with mental health disorders are at high risk of suicide and re-offending.

More than half of the children admitted to the juvenile correctional centers run by the state Office of Children and Family Services suffer from mental illness, according to the agency's own statistics. Independent experts put the number even higher. Some 72 percent of males and 87 percent of females in secure facilities nationwide have at least one mental health disorder, accord-ing to the Office of Juvenile Justice and Delinquency Prevention, part of the U.S. Department of Justice. "Children with serious mental illness may wind up in juvenile lock-ups even if the charges against them are relatively minor because there are so few alternatives for children who need psychiatric care" (Hemphill 2009).

Investigations by the Department of Justice found that staff members regularly used excessive force to restrain children, resulting in broken teeth, broken bones, and concussions. In addition, the Justice Department found that many facilities failed to provide adequate mental health care and treat-ment for seriously disturbed residents.

For example in one center, "the staff was 'at a loss' for how to address the problems of a girl who urinated and defecated on the floor of her room, refused medication, and stayed in her pajamas all day. She was isolated in a 'cottage' without other girls for three months. Another center had a boy who had an upsetting phone call from his family hurt himself by repeatedly rub-bing a scratch on his finger raw. The staff didn't know how to stop him—so they handcuffed him and took him to an emergency room" (Hemphill 2009).

Many studies indicate the juvenile justice system's difficulties in address-ing mental illness among youths such as: Inadequate and fragmented services for youths with mental health and substance abuse problems involved in the juvenile justice system.

Additionally, there are few programs specifically targeting the needs of youths in the juvenile justice system with cultural, racial, gender, sexual orientation, and developmental issues; there is a failure to provide routine standardized screening and assessments. Youths of color are frequently mis-diagnosed or not diagnosed at all, due to lack of communication and coordi-nation across the involved systems, such as schools, family and social service organizations, law enforcement agencies, and medical institutions.

Much needs to be done to improve and respond to the mental health needs of youths in the juvenile justice system. Some of these challenges are:

- Inadequate funding;
- Need for further research on juvenile justice and mental health programming;
- Sensitivity in mental health programming to vulnerable populations, especially minority and female offenders, who require specific services and treatment for special needs and certain risk factors;
- Involvement of youths and their families in community-based mental health treatments that serve, support. and supervise a child and family in an individualized way;
- Useful models and approaches for stimulating needed changes in policy, programs, and practice (Center for Children's Law and Policy: Building Blocks for Youth).

Laurence Steinberg in his work introduced four solutions that he put forth as a way to solve the problems of youths in the juvenile justice system. He proposed the following:

First—for youth in the community, family-based programs, such as Functional Family Therapy, Multisystemic Therapy, or Multidimensional Treatment Foster Care, are more consistently effective than those that focus on treating the individual juvenile alone.

Second—for youth in institutional settings, treatments that follow basic principles of cognitive-behavioral therapy are generally superior to those that take a different approach.

Third—programs that are excessively harsh or punitive, like boot camps, either have no effects or iatrogenic effects.

Fourth—incarceration in and of itself is an expensive proposition that yields little benefit other than the short-term effect of incapacitation; that is, incarceration has no lasting deterrent effect once a juvenile is released back into the community (www.princeton.edu).

As you can see he advocates for change and believes that without it there will be no quick solutions and that it must be a systematic process of implementation and a reflective and well thought out systems approach.

REHABILITATION AND TREATMENT
PROGRAMS THAT WORK

Even the best evidence-based programs must be correctly implemented to be effective (Grisso 2008). An extensive body of research has demonstrated the effectiveness of community-based rehabilitation and treatment programs for delinquent youth, including violent juvenile offenders. The critical components of successful programs for such youth are:

- Small size, so that youths can receive individualized attention;
- Intensive case management, with small case loads, to allow close supervision of youths and enable youths to develop positive relationships with adults;
- An emphasis on re-entry and re-integration into the home community through appropriate aftercare services;
- Opportunities for young people in the programs to make decisions and to achieve success;
- Clear and consistent consequences for misbehavior or violation of program rules;
- High-quality educational and vocational programming; and
- A variety of forms of individual and family counseling matched to particular needs of youth in the program (Center For Children's Law and Policy).

Juvenile detention centers are often at maximum capacity, understaffed, and resource poor. The criminal justice system continues to house youths in facilities that are not safe or downright dirty, and unhealthy. How can rehabilitation occur in places that are doomed and ineffective? The answer is it cannot help youths. In fact it just reinforces to youths, families, and community agencies the ineffectiveness of a control punishment system. Each state is at a different place in terms of juvenile detention reform.

The Juvenile Detention Prevention Reauthorization Act has begun its work in the area of reform. Below you will find the four areas of focus for the committee that has been charged with making juvenile detention centers more humanistic and effective places.

1. Combat overreliance on training school incarceration and pretrial detention. Juvenile justice systems routinely detain and incarcerate youths who pose little or no danger to public safety, despite research that community supervision and nonresidential, evidence-based programs are more effective and vastly more cost-efficient.
2. Take aggressive steps to reduce racial disparities in juvenile justice. Perhaps the most troubling characteristic of our nation's juvenile justice system is the shameful and persistent overrepresentation of minority youth. The research is now clear that youths of color are treated more harshly than white youths at every stage of the juvenile

process, even when they present the same histories and are accused of the same crimes.

3. Combat abuse and protect the safety of youths confined in juvenile facilities. Conditions of confinement within juvenile detention and corrections facilities are deeply problematic. Violence and abuse are rampant in many facilities, as are the excessive use of isolation and dangerous or overly harsh disciplinary techniques such as four-point restraints, strip searches, and pepper sprays. Juvenile systems in California, Texas, and several other states have been plunged into scandal in recent years by revelations of endemic abuse, and the Associated Press recently reported that 13,000 cases of abuse were reported in juvenile institutions nationwide from 2004 to 2007.

4. Limit the number of youths tried in adult courts. Brain studies and social science research now show conclusively that adolescents are less mature than adults (and therefore less culpable for their crimes), and more likely to desist from crime and respond to rehabilitation. Studies consistently find that young people prosecuted and punished in the adult justice system are more likely to reoffend than similar youths retained in the juvenile system. Nonetheless, an estimated 200,000 youthful offenders are tried in adult courts every year, many of whom are punished in adult prisons or probation/parole systems. Some live in states that define the age of juvenile jurisdiction at sixteen or seventeen, rather than eighteen, and many others are transferred to adult courts through ill-considered transfer and waiver laws passed in the 1990s (Juvenile Justice and Delinquency Prevention Act).

The important factor to remember is that youth violence is preventable and with the right kinds of supports or programs or resources juveniles can remain out of custody and make better choices. The Future of Children website has offered the following suggestions for prevention.

PREVENTION PROGRAMS

Primary prevention programs target the general population of youths and include efforts to prevent smoking, drug use, and teen pregnancy—and can be as far removed from juvenile delinquency as home visiting programs or quality preschool. Secondary prevention programs target youths at elevated risk for a particular outcome, such as delinquency or violence.

Programs to pay attention to are:

The David Olds Nurse Home Visitation Program: This program trains and supervises nurses who pay approximately twenty home visits to young, poor, first-time mothers. The results have been dramatic. There have been:

- Significant reduction of child abuse and neglect
- Lower arrest rates for children and mothers
- Decrease in welfare receipt
- Decrease in subsequent births (www.princeton.edu/.../publications/highlights/18_02_Highlights.pdf).

In addition, a high-quality preschool, modeled after the Perry Preschool in Ypsilanti, Michigan, is a structured and well-defined preschool program that emphasizes collaborative planning and problem solving among teachers, parents, students, community members, and administrators, which filters down to the students and the children in their care.

The fact that there are small class sizes where children receive sufficient adult attention enables children to be corrected and monitored more often and fully. Faculty receive ongoing continuing education and professional development to enhance their skills, which directly related to how these adults work on a day-to-day basis with these children.

Integrated curriculum and student involvement in rule setting and enforcement builds a sense of ownership and accountability for all. These interventions have been proven as great solutions to the prevention of later drug use, delinquency, anti-social behavior, and early school drop-out (www.princeton.edu/.../publications/highlights/18_02_Highlights.pdf).

The Bullying Prevention Program, Bergen, Norway, was designed for elementary and middle school students. The core components of the program revolve around parents and teachers setting and enforcing clear anti-bullying rules that were able to be taught and enforced at the school level. There was a decline in bullying by 50 percent two years after implementation and a decrease in other forms of delinquency (www.princeton.edu/futureofchildren/.../18_02_Highlights.pdf).

Life Skills Training: Classroom program to prevent substance abuse. There has been a proven reduction in the use of alcohol, cigarettes, and marijuana.

Project STATUS: School-based program aimed at junior and senior high school students to reduce delinquency and drop-out.

- Less delinquency
- Less drug use
- Less negative peer pressure
- Better student to student bonding

- Greater academic success (www.princeton.edu/.../publications/highlights/18_02_Highlights.pdf).

The School Transitional Environmental Program (STEP): STEP groups students who are at greatest risk for behavioral problems in homerooms where the teachers take on the additional role of guidance counselor. They offer:

- Decreased absenteeism and drop-out
- Increased academic success
- More positive feelings about school
  (www.princeton.edu/.../publications/highlights/18_02_Highlights.pdf).

COMMUNITY-BASED INTERVENTIONS

Juvenile justice community-based programs vary widely, from one-hour monthly meetings to intensive family therapy and services. Programs range from diverting youth out of the juvenile justice system to serving youth on probation to working with youth on parole after a residential placement.

The most effective community-based interventions are those that emphasize family interactions and build the skills of a juvenile's parents or other caretaker. The least effective are those that focus on the individual and/or punish and try to "scare straight" youth. For years there was a belief that if you had inmates scare youths they would not reoffend; the fact is that many of these offenders ended up in jail regardless of what they had been taught.

A program that has had some success is the Functional Family Therapy (FFT): The core components of this program are aimed at eleven- to eighteen-year-olds who are having problems with delinquency, substance abuse, or violence; this program focuses on improving family dynamics and family relationships and improving communication skills for all within the family unit. Individual therapists work with a family in the home to improve problem solving, increase emotional connections, and strengthen parents' abilities to provide structure, guidance, and limits for their children. The parents receive individual coaching and are supported in a variety of ways.

The program has received accolades as it has been well-documented for over twenty-five years and has been proven to be successful in changing family dynamics. This family therapy has shown that it works for a wide range of problem youths for all walks of life.

The list of effective therapists range from social work and counseling professionals to paraprofessionals and trainees that are invested in helping the family and youths be successful. They invest the time to teach the skills but also to monitor and support the family when needed.

One of the largest benefits of this program is that it is an easily transportable program that can go where the families are and work within a variety of communities.

Multisystemic Therapy (MST): A family-based program designed to help parents deal effectively with the behavioral problems of their adolescents, MST provides fifty hours of counseling with master-level professionals and round-the-clock crisis intervention over a four-month period. Results have shown that it reduces rearrests and out-of-home placements for problem youths in the juvenile justice and social services systems.

Intensive Protective Supervision (IPS): IPS is an alternative to the traditional parole officer model in that is more targeted at nonserious status offenders. The benefit of this program is that it enables case managers to interact with the teen and his or her family by making frequent home visits, offering support for parents, developing individual service plans, and arranging for services as needed. Typically the youth who best qualifies for this program is less likely to be referred to juvenile court for supervision and during the one year following and is more likely to have completed treatment overall.

INSTITUTIONAL SETTINGS

Institutions for juvenile offenders range from group homes to camps to residential or correction facilities. Research shows that there are three general strategies that improve effectiveness of out-of-home placements:

1. focusing on risk factors that can be changed, such as low skills, substance abuse, defiant behavior, and friendships with delinquent peers;
2. tailoring each program to the clients' needs; and
3. focusing interventions on higher-risk youth.
(www.princeton.edu/futureofchildren/.../18_02_Highlights.pdf).

It is extremely important that when a youth offender is recommended for out-of-home placements, all supporting evidence and documentation be collected by the case managers involved. An out-of-home placement needs to be well supported and hopefully the placement that will lead to the largest leaps in improvement.

Successful programs share common characteristics:

1. they are implemented with integrity;
2. they offer longer periods of intervention;

3. they are older, more established programs; and
4. they focus on treatment of mental health issues versus punishment. (www.princeton.edu/futureofchildren/.../18_02_Highlights.pdf).

It is imperative that out-of-home placements be institutions that have a proven record of success and are not just holding pens for troubled youth. They need to be well versed and invested in helping troubled youth become more productive members of society instead of rebels.

Specific programs that have been noted by researchers include:

- Cognitive Behavior Therapy (CBT): Focuses mainly on identifying life goals and developing skills to help them achieve them.
- Aggressive Replacement Training: Identifies risk factors that can be changed, focusing on anger control, behavioral/pro-social skills, and moral reasoning.
- Family Integrated Transitions (FIT): Designed for youths with mental health or substance abuse problems, this program uses behavioral and other therapies to help institutionalized youths reintegrate in the community.
- Multidimensional Treatment Foster Care (MTFC): MTFC is modeled after the foster care system, except that the MTFC foster parents are paid higher rates and expected to do more—be at home when the teen is at home, complete training that teaches behavior management, attend weekly group meetings, and engage in daily supportive telephone calls with MTFC staff. Aimed at delinquent youths who would otherwise qualify for group home placement, evaluations show that while MTFC costs more than traditional group homes, it is more effective in reducing arrest rates so produces savings to the criminal justice system and to potential victims (Grisso 2008).

In conclusion, juvenile detention centers have a long way to go to become places that are youth focused, humanistic, and respectful. It is very true that the population that they receive are not model citizens; however, where else are these youths going to learn to become better citizens? Are they so damaged that we just lock them up until they become adults and transfer them to adult prisons? The amount of wasted talent and potential is in the billions of dollars. We need to improve at preventing children and youths from entering the juvenile justice system. The only way we will do that is to make our children a priority and guide them very carefully as they develop into hopefully honest, productive and law abiding citizens. We can only hope that we do not lose too many from birth to adulthood.

7

Juvenile Prison System Experience

We all know that prisons are a place of containment. Such institutions throughout America are plentiful and full. Adult prisons are places of fear, intimidation, and crime. The adults that are incarcerated there are there for a multiple of reasons. There are very few innocent individuals locked up. This chapter will investigate the juvenile experience in juvenile detention centers as well as in adult prisons.

YOUTH CRIME

Youths commit only a small portion of the nation's crime. For example, "in 2008, 12% of violent crime clearances and 18% of the property crime clearances nationwide involved only youth" (FBI 2009). According to the FBI, "youth under age 18 accounted for 15% of all arrests" (FBI 2009). Youth crime rates have been declining for many years. "The number of adults arrested in 2008 and in 1999 increased 3.4%, whereas the number of juveniles arrested dropped a staggering 15.7% during that same time frame" (FBI 2008).

The statistics inform us that youth crime is in decline yet the media is creating havoc when there is a crime committed by a juvenile. It makes national news and the activists for juvenile reform and justice become louder and demand more sanctions and programs for troubled youths.

YOUTH IN THE JUVENILE JUSTICE SYSTEM

"More than 31 million youth were under juvenile court jurisdiction in 2007. Of these youth, 79% were between the ages of 10 and 15, 12% were age 16 and 9% were age 17." The fact that the largest proportion of youth offenders are between this age does indicate that children and teens are acting out earlier and becoming involved with the juvenile justice system at a much earlier age then previous generations.

The statistics also noted that the fact that there was a rather small proportion of 16- and 17-year-olds among the juvenile court population is related to the upper age of juvenile court jurisdiction, which varies by state. In one state you may be classified as an adult and in another still under juvenile jurisdiction. "In 2007, youth age 16 in 3 states were under the original jurisdiction of the criminal court, as were youth age 17 in an additional 10 states" (www .campaignforyouthjustice.org/.../FS_KeyYouthCrimeFacts.pdf).

"Although more 17-year-olds than 16-year-olds were arrested in 2009 (456,000 compared to 405,800), the number of juvenile court cases involving 17-year-olds (312,000) was lower than the number involving 16-year-olds (417,400). The explanation lies primarily in the fact that in 13 states, 17-year olds are excluded from original jurisdiction of the juvenile court and are considered adults" (www.campaignforyouthjustice.org/.../FS_KeyYouthCrimeFacts .pdf).

"In 2008, 22% of arrests involving youth who were eligible in their State for processing in the juvenile justice system, were handled within law enforcement agencies and the youth were released, 66% were referred to juvenile court, and 10% were referred directly to criminal court" (Puzzanchera, Adams, and Sickmund 2010). There does not seem to be any type of consistency throughout the different parts of the United States when it comes with dealing with upper level youths. Would it be a more effective system if it became a federal jurisdiction when dealing with youth offenders?

JUVENILE COURT

"Every year, juvenile courts in the U.S. handle an estimated 1.7 million cases in which the youth was charged with a delinquency offense" (Puzzanchera, Adams, and Sickmund 2010). "In 2007, juvenile courts handled about 4,600 delinquency cases per day" (Puzzanchera, Adams, and Sickmund 2010). "The trends in juvenile court cases paralleled the decline in arrests of persons younger than 18. The number of juvenile court cases involving offenses included in the FBI's Violent Crime Index (criminal homicide, forcible rape, robbery, and aggravated assault) declined 9% between 1998 and 2007" (Puzzanchera, Adams, and Sickmund 2010).

JUVENILE DETENTION AND CORRECTIONS

"In 2008, there were fewer than 81,000 juvenile offenders removed from their homes and held in residential placement (e.g., juvenile detention facilities, corrections facilities, group homes or shelters) on one day, the fewest count since 1993" (Sickmund 2010).

After arrest, many youth are detained in a detention or other residential facility to await a hearing in juvenile or adult court, depending on how they are charged. While in out-of-home placement, youth are separated from their community and their normal day-to-day life (school, jobs, family, etc.). "Every day, there are over 26,000 youth who are detained in America" (Sickmund et al. 2008). "One out of every 5 youth (22%) who is brought before the court with a delinquency case is detained" (Puzzanchera, Adams, and Sickmund 2010).

"Detention facilities are meant to temporarily house youth who are likely to commit another crime before their trial or who are likely to skip their court date." It is a known fact that many of the "youth held in the 591 detention centers across the country do not meet these criteria and should not be there" (Holman and Ziedenberg 2006). Again there is no efficiency or effectiveness in the system when there are whole groups of youths who would be better served or held in another facility than in an institution where the most troubled are kept.

"Most detained youth are held in locked 'secure' settings such as a juvenile detention facility. Of these youth, 83% are confined by three or more locks during the day (e.g., youth are locked within buildings, within areas within buildings, and within external fences or walls)" (Sedlack and McPherson 2010). The interesting fact is that many are not dangerous and therefore do not need to be contained to this level. Is this an overreaction of the system?

"More than two-thirds of youth in detention are held for nonviolent charges. These youth are charged with property offenses, drug offenses, public order offenses, technical probation violations, or status offenses (crimes that wouldn't be crimes if they were adults, like running away or breaking curfew)" (Sickmund 2008). The fact that many of these actions or behaviors are not severe enough to warrant this level of intervention the juvenile justice system lashes out with as a way of intervening. The system is using a club when a more creative measure should be used.

It is very obvious that there is an overuse of detention for youth of color. "African-American youth are detained at a rate 4.5 times higher than whites. Latino youth are detained at twice the rate of whites" (Holman and

Ziedenberg 2006). "One quarter (25%) of detention centers are at or over their capacity, which impairs the ability of the facility to properly care for the youth" (Livsey, Sickmund, and Sladky 2009).

A one-day snapshot of juvenile offenders in detention found that "roughly 3% were status offenders" (Sickmund et al. 2008). However, one often does not see the inclusion of those offenders who are in violation of parole or have their case waiting to be heard.

"Nearly one-fifth of the less serious career offenders (status offenders, technical parole violators, and youth who report no offense) are placed in living units with youth who have killed someone, and about one-fourth reside with felony sex offenders" (Sedlack and McPherson 2010).

After adjudication, youths are sentenced to correctional institutions or to some level of residential state school or facility. "On any given day, nearly 65,000 youth are placed by the court into an out-of-home placement. Approximately half of these youth (27,000) are committed to an incarceration facility such as a state training school" (Sickmund et al. 2008).

There are less severe alternatives to incarcerating youth, and they work. Community-based programs, including diversion programs, drug treatment, evening reporting centers, treatment clinics and family programs, have been shown to be less costly than detention or incarceration and to help youth stay out of trouble and to not re-offend (Juvenile Detention Alternatives Initiative 2007).

Confined youth are at great risk of sexual assault. "More than 1 in 10 youth (12%) in state juvenile facilities and large nonstate facilities reported experiencing one or more incidents of sexual victimization by another youth or facility staff in the past 12 months or since admission, if less than 12 months" (Beck, Harrison, and Guerino 2010). It is a well-known fact that youths are at risk of sexual victimization and will rarely escape placement without having had some personal experience with this issue. It is much more common than what is reported. Many youths do not report because of fear of reprisals or additional victimizations.

"One-fifth of youth in juvenile facilities are in living units with others who are 3 or more years older than they are. In fact, 43% of juveniles in placement are housed in living units with young adults" (Sedlack and McPherson 2010). "Youth under the age of 18 who are in units with young adults are more than twice as likely as juveniles not living in units with young adults (42% compared to 20%) to be living with youth whose most serious career offense is murder" (Sedlack and McPherson 2010). The placement of dangerous offenders with minor offenders only leads to a system of hierarchy that is founded in violence and control. The losers are often the less violent offenders who become the targets.

YOUTH IN THE ADULT CRIMINAL JUSTICE SYSTEM

An estimated 200,000 youth are tried, sentenced, or incarcerated as adults every year across the United States (Woolard 2005) Most of the youth prosecuted in adult court are charged with nonviolent offenses (Campaign for Youth Justice 2007). Research shows that young people who are kept in the juvenile justice system are less likely to reoffend than young people who are transferred into the adult system.

According to the Centers for Disease Control and Prevention, "youth who are transferred from the juvenile court system to the adult criminal system are approximately 34% more likely than youth retained in the juvenile court system to be re-arrested for violent or other crime" (CDC 2007). "Youth sentenced as adults receive an adult criminal record, are often denied employment and educational opportunities, and can be barred from receiving student financial aid" (National Prison Rape Elimination Commission 2009). In these cases the future looks incredibly bleak and the chances of having success in the outside world diminishes greatly, which may lead to the youth offending again as a way of managing on the streets.

HOUSING YOUTH IN THE ADULT SYSTEM IN ADULT JAILS AND PRISONS

Although federal law requires that youth in the juvenile justice system be removed from adult jails or be sight-and-sound separated from other adults, these protections do not apply to youth prosecuted in the adult criminal justice system. These youths are treated like adult criminals and must suffer the consequences of their actions as adults.

For years there has been a debate as to what to do with young people who are sentenced to adult jails. Many people who have worked within these adult jails often face a dangerous dilemma, they must choose between housing youth in the general adult population where they are at substantial risk of physical and sexual abuse, or housing youth in segregated settings in which isolation can cause or exacerbate mental health problems.

Youth who are held in adult facilities are at the greatest risk of sexual victimization. The National Prison Rape Elimination Commission (2009) found that "more than any other group of incarcerated persons, youth incarcerated with adults are probably at the highest risk for sexual abuse." Many children are often placed in isolation which can produce harmful consequences. Youth are frequently locked down twenty-three hours a day in small cells with no natural light.

These conditions can cause anxiety and paranoia, exacerbate existing mental disorders, and put youth at risk of suicide. For example, youth housed in adult jails are thirty-six times more likely to commit suicide than are youth housed in juvenile detention facilities (Jailing Juveniles 2007).

"On any given day, nearly 7,500 young people are locked up in adult jails" (Jailing Juveniles 2007). It is my belief that these numbers are probably much increased in 2011. Currently, "39 states permit or require that youth charged as adults be held before they are tried in an adult jail. In some states, if they are convicted, they may be required to serve their entire sentence in an adult jail" (Jailing Juveniles 2007). "A significant portion of youth detained in adult jails before their trial are not convicted as adults. One-half of these youth will be sent back to the juvenile justice system and/or not be convicted at all. Yet, most of these youth will have spent at least one month in an adult jail and one in five of these youth will have spent over six months in an adult jail" (Jailing Juveniles 2007).

According to research by the Bureau of Justice Statistics, "youth under the age of 18 represented 21 percent of all substantiated victims of inmate-on-inmate sexual violence in jails in 2005, and 13 percent in 2006—surprisingly high since only one percent of jail inmates are juveniles" (Beck, Harrison, and Adams 2007).

"On any given day, more than 3,600 young people are locked up in adult prisons" (West 2009). Deborah LaBelle, an attorney working with over 400 youth serving sentences of life without possibility of parole, testified before the National Prison Rape Elimination Commission "that 80 percent of those youth had been sexually assaulted within the first year of their incarceration in adult prisons" (Labelle 2005).

The majority of youth held in adult prisons are likely to be released in early adulthood. "Approximately 80 percent of youth convicted as adults will be released from prison before their 21st birthday, and 95 percent will be released before their 25th birthday" (Redding 2008). At the other extreme, we know that some young people incarcerated in adult prisons will expect to spend the majority of their lifetimes behind bars. Human Rights Watch reported in 2009 "that an estimated 2,600 people were serving life without parole for crimes they committed while under age 18" (Human Rights Watch 2009).

RACIAL AND ETHNIC DISPARITIES

Youth of color are overrepresented at all stages in the juvenile justice system, according to the National Council on Crime and Delinquency, in their January 2007 report "And Justice for Some." "African-American youth overwhelmingly receive harsher treatment than white youth in the juvenile justice system at most stages of case processing. African-American youth make up 30% of those arrested while they only represent 17% of the overall youth population. At the other extreme end of the system, African-American youth are 62% of the youth prosecuted in the adult criminal system and are nine times more likely than white youth to receive an adult prison sentence" (Arya and Augarten 2008). The juvenile system in America seems to be readily available to ethnic minorities. Is this a case of a prejudiced society that does not give opportunity to disenfranchised youth? Why do not all youths in America have an equal chance at being successful?

Compared to white youth, "Latino youth are 4% more likely to be petitioned, 16% more likely to be adjudicated delinquent, 28% more likely to be detained, and 41% more likely to receive an out-of-home placement." The Latino youth are more likely to have been part of a gang and therefore seem to be destined to be part of the adult system. Once in the adult system they are "43% more likely than white youth to be waived to the adult system and 40% more likely to be admitted to adult prison" (Arya et al. 2009).

Native youth are more likely to receive severe punishments in the juvenile justice systems: "out-of-home placement (i.e., incarceration in a state correctional facility) and waiver to the adult system. Compared to white youth, Native youth are 1.5 times more likely to receive out-of-home placement and are 1.5 times more likely to be waived to the adult criminal system." "Nationwide, the average rate of new commitments to adult state prison for Native youth is 1.84 times that of white youth" (Arya and Rolnick 2008). This confirms yet again that American society is discriminatory toward youth of color. Why the difference? Why such inequality of justice? My belief is that there are two Americas, one for the whites and one for everyone else.

FAMILY INVOLVEMENT

"The ability of family members to meaningfully participate in their children's lives makes a dramatic difference on youth outcomes. The overwhelming majority (94%) of youth want to maintain contact with their family" (Sedlack and McPherson 2010). The frequency of family contact varies significantly by type of program that youth are involved in.

Many youth who are incarcerated are unable to have regular contact with family. "Thirty-nine percent of corrections and camp youth have family contact less than once a week" (Sedlack and McPherson 2010). "One third of youth who have no in-person visits indicate that this is due to time constraints or distance. In fact, the majority of all youth in custody (59%) say that it would take their families 1 hour or longer to travel to visit them. For more than one-fourth of youth (28%), their families would have to travel 3 hours or longer to see them" (Sedlack and McPherson 2010). Not only are these youths separated from their families but they are also cut off emotionally from anyone who may offer any type of encouragement or support that may help the youth cope with their incarceration. The youth is isolated once again and more likely to act out due to having no personal connection with significant others.

COST-EFFECTIVE ALTERNATIVES

"Incarcerating young people in juvenile detention facilities costs between $32,000 and $65,000 per year and operating just one bed over a twenty-year period can cost between $1.25 million and $1.5 million" (National Association of Counties 2007). Alternatives to incarcerating youth not only reduce crime, but save money. Research has shown that every dollar spent on evidence-based programs [e.g., Multidimensional Treatment Foster Care (MTFC), Multisystemic Therapy (MST), and Functional Family Therapy (FFT)] can yield up to $13 in cost savings (Juvenile Detention Alternatives Initiative 2007).

"Early interventions that prevent high-risk youth from engaging in repeat criminal offenses can save the public nearly $5.7 million in costs over a lifetime" (Cohen and Piquero 2007). The cost savings to early intervention is a great investment into America's youth. Why are we not doing it more frequently when problems arise? The answers are numerous: a false sense of optimism hoping that the problem will get better, lack of services, and lack of accurate reporting and evaluations.

PUBLIC VIEWS ON YOUTH CRIME AND THE JUSTICE SYSTEM

According to a 2007 nationwide Zogby poll, commissioned by the National Council on Crime and Delinquency, "91% of Americans believe that increasing counseling and substance abuse treatment through the juvenile justice system will help reduce crime" (Attitudes of US Voters 2007). That same 2007 Zogby poll reported that "89% of Americans believe rehabilitative services and treatment for incarcerated youth can help prevent future crimes."

CRADLE TO PRISON PIPELINE

It is sad to see that the conditions in which a child is born may determine whether he or she will become victims or criminals. The incidence of children being involved in crime if they are born in poverty is extremely high. These children come from low income neighborhoods that are often already rifled with crime. The children learn from the modeling they observe on a daily basis. The opportunities to engage in criminal activity are never very far away. Children as young as five to six years of age are already involved in activities way beyond their developmental capacities.

Race and poverty seem to be the magic combination that seems to create children more likely to enter the juvenile correctional system. Depressed neighborhoods, low performing schools, and lack of afterschool activities are also seen as contributing to the likelihood of juvenile crime. Many of these children do not have access to health care, nor did their mothers while they were pregnant, as prenatal care is often nonexistent in many of these communities. The sad part is that there seems to be almost thirty million people in America who do not have access to health care.

It is easy to surmise that without health care women who give birth to children with problems cannot get the services they require, such as vaccinations, ongoing health checkups, and any type of assistance if the mother used drugs or alcohol during pregnancy. These children are victims from birth. Many of these children have attention deficit disorders, posttraumatic disorders, personality disorders, learning disabilities, and low cognitive functioning, which make them unlikely to be successful in a school environment. Being unsuccessful in a school environment often leads to early expulsion or acting out behaviors that are partnered with emotional and behavior disorders.

Many children who live in poverty are living in families headed by single mothers who may not have the ability to care for their children because of low paying jobs, no health care, and no existing support systems. This leaves them in a situation where they are just able to be at a survival level. These individuals often do not have the ability to provide necessary stimulation for their children, putting their children even more at risk of beginning school already delayed cognitively and academically.

Early childhood education is a key to reversing the damage done in the early years of life for many of these children who become juvenile delinquents. The public school system needs to provide extensive support services for these children. Parents need to have access to quality child-care settings, including excellent early year teachers and programs that build skills and are flexible enough to adapt to the needs of this very specialized population.

These educators must be able to analyze and program for the developmental and learning difficulties that these children are arriving with when they come to school. There needs to be more ethnically diverse teachers teaching in these low socially economic schools. Children need to be understood from both a racial and an ethnic point of view.

The school system and many of its policies often create more chaos in these communities because of the expectations that are developed. In many of the low performing schools there is an abundance of violence. In their efforts to control the violence school districts have created zero tolerance policies that accomplish one thing, they put kids on the street to create more crime.

Zero tolerance policies work well for many middle and upper level communities as a deterrent from criminal activity; however in lower level communities zero tolerance policies create more juvenile crimes. It may be time to reexamine these policies and think outside of the box so that these children and youth receive the services they need to become productive members of society instead of another statistic that costs more money in the long run because of having to cage them up.

There are many youths who do serious crimes and need to be removed from the schools; however, if one looks at the statistics, most youths expelled from school are expelled for misdemeanors, such as fighting, bullying, harassment, and drug and alcohol infractions. The school system has a zero tolerance policy but also has become the most prominent supplier of the pipeline of schoolhouse to jailhouse for many youths.

The last component of the cradle to prison pipeline is the foster child system. Many of the children who live in families or communities that are marginalized often end up running away from home, attack their siblings or parents, or commit petty crimes. They are often removed because of neglect, abuse, both physical and sexual, and for refusal to attend school. In an earlier chapter in this book the foster care system was examined and the findings were quite conclusive that this system creates more victims and more juvenile criminals than it takes care of in the long run.

The foster care system is another direct pipeline to the prison system because youths are disenfranchised, not connected to supportive families, communities, and services, and are often left to their own devices to survive. The foster care system may have good intentions but they are often underfunded, understaffed, and their resources are limited. The supply of services cannot meet the demand, so therefore many become the statistics highlighted earlier in this chapter.

The following have been highlighted as programs that are making some headway in changing the direction of the cradle to prison pipeline.

Model Programs Making a Difference

Harlem Children's Zone is a community-based organization that works to enhance the quality of life for children and families in a sixty-block area of Central Harlem. Its mission "is to create significant positive opportunities for all children by helping parents, residents and teachers create a safe learning environment for youth" (www.hcz.org).

Boston Ten Point Coalition

This ecumenical group of Christian clergy and lay leaders works to mobilize the Christian community around issues affecting black and Latino youth, especially those at-risk for violence, drug abuse, and other destructive behaviors (www.bostontenpoint.org).

Comer School Development Program

This program is run by the Yale Child Study Center; this school reform model is centered on children's growth along six developmental pathways: cognitive, physical, psychological, ethical, social, and linguistic. This approach is designed to compensate for children growing up in families unable to provide them with adequate developmental experiences (www.schooldevelopment-program.org).

The PACE Center for Girls

This is a school-based and gender-responsive program that began in Florida as an alternative to incarceration. It focuses on understanding the relationship between victimization and female juvenile crime and developing the unique potential of each girl (www.pacecenter.org).

Operation Ceasefire

This is a national model for effective and dramatic youth and gang violence reduction through the efforts of a broad coalition of federal, state, and local governmental agencies, nonprofit community service organizations, businesses, religious leaders, parents, and residents. John Jay College of Criminal Justice is a national leader in implementing the Ceasefire model in multiple jurisdictions across the country (dakennedy@jjay.cuny.edu).

Children's Defense Fund Freedom Schools

This is an after-school and summer program committed to instilling love and learning in children in kindergarten through 12th grade living in high-need communities. Students participate in activities and field trips that develop their minds and bodies and nurture their spirits (www.freedomschools.org).

MENTAL HEALTH

Jails and juvenile justice facilities are the new asylums. Children and youths are finding their way into the juvenile justice system because of the lack of services or supports. As cash-starved states slash mental health programs in communities and schools, they are increasingly relying on the juvenile corrections system to handle a generation of young offenders with psychiatric disorders. About two-thirds of the nation's juvenile inmates have at least one mental illness, according to surveys of youth prisons, and are more in need of therapy than punishment.

Juveniles with mental health and other specialized needs are overrepresented in the juvenile justice system, and while juvenile corrections have not historically provided standardized and evidence-based mental health services for its incarcerated youth, the demand is evident. The reality is that juveniles with serious mental illness are committed to youth corrections facilities, and justice systems generally do not have the capacity to provide effective mental health care.

Here is an example of an Ohio teen's experience:

> The teenager in the padded smock sat in his solitary confinement cell here in this state's most secure juvenile prison and screamed obscenities. The youth, Donald, a freckle-faced 16-year-old, his eyes glassy from lack of sleep and a daily regimen of mood stabilizers, was serving six months for stealing a gun. Although he had received diagnoses for psychiatric illnesses, including bipolar disorder, a judge decided that Donald would get better care in the state correctional system than he could get anywhere in his county. That was two years ago. Donald's confinement has been repeatedly extended because of his violent outbursts. This year he assaulted a guard at the prison, the Ohio River Valley Juvenile Correctional Facility, and was charged anew, with assault. His fists and forearms are striped with scars where he gouged himself with pencils and the bones of a bird he caught and dismembered. (Moore 2009)

The research has been very good at predicting that the populations most at risk in a juvenile detention center with mental health issues are females and minority children. Females are often victims of abuse, trauma, mood disorders, and life circumstances that often have left them unable to deal with life's challenges and have resorted to drug, alcohol, or sexually acting out behaviors. They are the most vulnerable of the incarcerated youths. They often are able to access mental health services or these services have been minimized and the young female offender does not receive any type of treatment.

Minority juvenile offenders are plentiful in the system as explained earlier in this chapter. Because of their overrepresentation in the population their sheer numbers, the lack of ethnic support personnel and lack of services contributes to more acting out on the part of the youth and encourages the joining and attachment to the gang culture.

In the past most services were delivered through community or residential placements but because of the shift to having more incarcerated youth in juvenile detention centers these youths are not having access to these services as they are not abundant enough in the actual detention setting.

Juvenile corrections play a significant role in coordinating the juvenile justice and mental health systems of care in the provision of treatment services for these youth. The reality is that juveniles with serious mental illness are committed to youth corrections facilities, and these facilities must develop the capacity to provide effective mental health care.

Efficient mental health care requires that a system be put into place that supports case management and treatment interventions. There have been very few in-depth studies that extensively show how to use the juvenile justice system's limited resources. The individuals who provide this type of services must really be cognizant of the youths they work with. They have to have an excellent understanding of the skills and strengths the youth have, along with the skills that are lacking. The youth workers must also be competent in providing appropriate interventions for the management and treatment of this population (Underwood et al. 2006).

Juveniles with mental health disorders comprise a heterogeneous population with varying degrees and manifestations of mental illness. This has added to the difficulty in addressing mental health issues. Part of this intricacy is the multiple uses and definitions of the term mental health disorders. However, a distinction may be drawn between youth with serious mental illness and youth with serious emotional disturbances. The youths with serious mental illness will have cognitive and psychological impairments that have a clinical diagnosis (mood disorders, schizophrenia, anxiety disorders, etc.) while those with emotional disturbances usually have severe behavioral and coping skills issues.

The juvenile with serious mental illness poses the greatest challenge to juvenile correctional administrators and staff. "Youth with serious mental health issues require multiple services and supports. These necessary services may include: medications, intensive services for acuity, substance abuse treatment, and educational services" (Underwood et al. 2004).

HOW ARE MENTAL HEALTH DISORDERS CLASSIFIED?

Mental health issues and behavioral issues are not always fully clearly articulated and/or defined. In the youth system there is a very high need for a flexible diagnostic classification approach; it is necessary in distinguishing between the mental health and juvenile justice issues and implementing treatment strategies to deal with both sets of issues. "Antisocial and/or aggressive behavior is often mistaken as serious mental health disorders, when, in fact, there may be no manifestations of serious mental illness or it coexists with the antisocial and/or aggressive behavior" (Underwood et al. 2006).

CATEGORIES OF JUVENILES WITH MENTAL HEALTH DISORDERS

To lessen the confusion between definitional and diagnostic concerns Lee Underwood proposed a categorical approach to mental health. "Juveniles with mental health disorders who enter the juvenile justice system are different in terms of demographics, personal histories, personality functioning, and manifestations of mental disorders. When planning mental health services for these youth, it is important for juvenile justice administrators to have a framework based on the range of mental health disorders so that the appropriate treatment addresses the unique needs of each youth" (Underwood et al. 2006).

The following section is presented to distinguish between six categories of mental health disorders that are common among the juveniles in the juvenile justice system. Each group of disorders has unique behavioral symptoms that pose as challenges to the treatment and management of juveniles in the justice system.

These indicators must be addressed by providing mental health interventions tailored to the individual, so that more comprehensive treatment can be implemented for the purpose of reducing the risk of future mental health crisis and criminal behavior (Underwood et al. 2006).

Mood and Affective Disorders

Affective disorders are common among juvenile offenders, ranking closely behind conduct and alcohol dependence disorders. When working with juveniles with affective disorders, it is important to be aware of the following alterations in mood and behavior.

1. Depressive states, co-occurring with conduct disorders, increase suicidal ideations and behavior.
2. Shifting mood states, from elevation to depression within brief periods, often occur without obvious provocation and are unpredictable.
3. Experiences feelings of agitation and irritability.
4. Exhibits spontaneous episodes of anger.

5. Engages in high risk behaviors.
6. Disinterest in daily activities resulting in social isolation and withdrawal often increases apathy.
7. Hopelessness and helplessness accompanied with an "I don't care" outlook on life are symptoms of depressed mood states.
8. Resist pharmacological management or seek inappropriate levels of medication in order to dull mood states (Underwood et al. 2006).

Anxiety disorders can manifest themselves in terms of phobias, obsessive compulsive actions, fears, worry, and agitation. The following list of symptoms may enable the working professional to understand that an anxiety disorder is at the root of the behavior. When working with juveniles with anxiety disorders, it is important to be aware of the following alterations in their anxiety and their behavior:

1. Limit testing behavior with the goal of diminishing internal conflict which emanates from the anticipation of danger.
2. Increased agitation occurs during periods of unrest in their environment. These juveniles tend to mimic the mood and tension levels of their peers and staff.
3. Increased agitation around bedtime which may stem from intruding thoughts of being abused in the past.
4. During heightened states of anxiety, these juveniles may be very difficult to manage as they may episodically exhibit panic or dissociation.
5. Anxiety can mimic physical symptoms. Availability of medical staff is necessary.
6. Anxiety and depression co-existing together is common which results in a greater risk for suicidal behavior.
7. Ruminative thinking that can generate more anxiety (Underwood et al. 2006).

Psychotic-Based Disorders

Psychotic disorders refer to a disintegration of thinking processes, affecting cognitive function perception, judgment, and mood as defined in clinical terms. These disorders are often manifested in an inability to distinguish external reality from internal beliefs. "Juveniles with psychotic disorders may experience poor reality testing, hallucinations, delusions, paranoia, social withdrawal, and ideas of reference. Disorganized speech and psychomotor disturbance are also common. These juveniles may have significant histories of bizarre experiences" (Underwood et al. 2006).

When working with juveniles with psychotic disorders, it is important to be aware of the following alterations in their thought and their behavior:

1. Juveniles in an active psychotic episode should be probated to community psychiatric facilities as soon as possible.
2. Adjustment to the correctional facility will be extremely difficult and if possible, removal from the facility to a psychiatric center is optimal.
3. Poor pharmacological management due to denying the existence and intensity of their problems is part of the symptomatology.
4. Teasing and victimizing behaviors exhibited by peers and staff due to their ignorance of the illness is common.
5. Frequent talking with oneself and arguing with unseen individuals is characteristic of psychosis.
6. Brief outbursts of terror which may be closely followed by eruptions of inappropriate laughter should not be confused with acting-out behavior.
7. Unprovoked impulsive behaviors that can range from low level impulsivity to acts of violence may occur (Underwood et al. 2006).

Co-Occurring Mental Health Disorders

Co-occurring disorders refer to the simultaneous experience of a substance use (abuse or dependence) and a mental disorder. "A diagnosis of co-occurring disorders occurs when at least one disorder of each type can be determined independent of the other and is not a cluster of symptoms resulting from the other disorder" (Miller et al. 1995).

These disorders have pronounced effects on the thoughts, mood, and behaviors of juveniles. Juveniles with co-occurring disorders often have histories of deeply rooted mental health issues for which the substance use allows temporary relief of emotional pain. "Juveniles with co-occurring disorders may also be more impulsive and potentially more violent than youth with an isolated mental health or substance use disorder. Often both the mental health and substance use issue are unrecognized and described by others as 'acting out' behavior. These youth often fall between the cracks due to mislabeling and failing to recognize their unique and specific needs" (Underwood et al. 2006).

When working with juveniles with co-occurring disorders, it is important for staff members to receive the following prerequisite training:

1. Cross-training in mental health and substance use disorders to fully understand each disorder, along with the co-occurring nature of the disorders is essential.
2. Dynamics of drug-seeking behavior as well as medical complications.

3. Symptom presentation may shift from signs of depression and anxiety to withdrawal.
4. Modulated therapeutic confrontations according to the fragility of the mental status of the juvenile (Underwood et al. 2006).

Personality-Based Disorders

"Personality disorders and traits refer to ingrained pervasive patterns of functioning that affect cognition, perception, mood, and behavior. The impact of these disorders affects the behavior of juveniles as they experience difficulties that are deeply rooted in their personality. These disorders involve underlying features of personality and may not necessarily be pathological, although certain style may cause interpersonal problems. These disorders are rigid, inflexible, and maladaptive and can often cause functional impairment and subjective distress (Underwood et al. 2006).

Juveniles with personality disorders and traits are difficult to manage and treat because the very existence of the disorder is often based in very difficult relationships and early developmental experiences.

When working with juveniles with personality disorders, it is important to be aware of the following personality alterations as well as management issues:

1. Behaviors may appear totally unrelated to the primary mental health diagnoses.
2. Behaviors may appear spontaneous and natural.
3. Juveniles do not consider the impact of their behaviors on others due to the pervasive nature of the disorders and traits.
4. Behaviors, which are integral to the juvenile's way of life, pose serious obstacles to treatment. Staff must understand that these behaviors change slowly.
5. Symptom substitution including other compulsive, manipulative, covert, and acting out behaviors is common (Underwood et al. 2006).

It is important to note "that juvenile offenders with mental health disorders will rarely display sole features of the aforementioned categories" (Ries 1994). Combinations of behaviors, based upon their experiences of life, are manifested differently in each juvenile. One cannot make the common mistake that there is a preset predetermined profile for these youths.

Disruptive Behavior-Based Disorders

Disruptive behavior disorders refer to a cluster of law-breaking and intrusive and invasive behaviors, often evidenced by disorderly conduct and aggression. Juveniles with disruptive behavior disorders are impulsive and have anxiety disorders. They often may have histories of criminal behaviors. "Destruction of property, deceitfulness, and aggressive acts are often experienced in the course of these disorders. Genetic and biological factors may significantly contribute to the onset of symptoms" (Underwood et al. 2006).

When working with juveniles with disruptive behavior disorders, it is important to be aware of the following alterations in mood and behavior.

1. Certain behaviors are exhibited in the attempt to dull or mask underlying emotional issues.
2. Adversarial relationships and negative attention seeking behavior is often preferred by juveniles with these disorders.
3. They often have limited problem solving skills.
4. Radically different ways of perceiving relationships is common.
5. Self-serving views of the world with the inability to understand the concept of injury to others is characteristic.
6. Use of power tactics and manipulative behaviors with peers and staff members are often common and perpetuate adversarial relationships.
7. The expression of anger is usually an attempt to re-channel underlying fears and anxieties (Underwood et al. 2006).

Neurologically Based Disorders

"Many disorders can be considered neurologically-based if they limit intellectual functioning include mental retardation, learning disorders, motor skills disorder, communication disorders, pervasive development disorders, attention-deficit/hyperactivity disorders (ADHD/ADD), feeding and eating disorders, tic disorders, and elimination disorders. Many behaviors displayed by juvenile offenders with neurological disorders can be misinterpreted especially those with ADHD/ADD" (Underwood et al. 2006).

When working with juveniles with ADHD/ADD, it is important to consider the following:

1. Disruptive behaviors of juveniles with ADHD/ADD may not be willful and may be the result of their disorder.
2. The longer ADHD/ADD symptoms go untreated, the more likely the individual will progress into criminal behavior.
3. Even if juveniles with ADHD/ADD want to control their actions, their behaviors can still be inconsistent and unpredictable.
4. Juveniles with ADHD/ADD do not respond well to repetitive, effortful, tedious activities that others choose for them.

5. Many juveniles with ADHD/ADD have a low threshold for arousal and are easily provoked.
6. Juveniles with ADHD/ADD need immediate, frequent, predictable, and meaningful rewards.
7. Juveniles with ADHD/ADD are at a higher risk for depression and other mood disorders

(Underwood et al. 2006).

• • •

This section on mental health issues is not comprehensive but an introduction in the world of these troubled individuals. On many occasions these youth with mental health issues do not get the help they need to truly understand or cope with their time behind bars. They have committed an act of violence or a crime and must be made accountable; however, is prison the answer or is it a mental health facility? The answer is individual and a system of juvenile corrections must begin looking at individuals rather than youth who commit this type of crime. It will be a long time before the system becomes conscious of individual need and individuality.

DEATH PENALTY

Currently, thirty-eight states authorize the death penalty; twenty-three of these permit the execution of offenders who committed capital offenses prior to their eighteenth birthdays. However, the laws governing application of the death penalty in those twenty-three states vary, and the variation is not necessarily tied to rates of juvenile crime. Since 1973, when the death penalty was reinstated, seventeen men have been executed for crimes they committed as juveniles and seventy-four people in the United States currently sit on death row for crimes they committed as juveniles (Streib 2000).

The debate as to the effectiveness of the death penalty to deterring crimes is still very strong and the evidence is still to be collected. The death penalty is used so rarely for juveniles due to public outcry that I do not see this as a viable alternative to crime or juvenile delinquency reduction.

Debate about the use of the death penalty for juveniles has grown more intense in light of calls for the harsher punishment of serious and violent juvenile offenders, changing perceptions of public safety, and international challenges to the death penalty's legality. Proponents see its use as a deterrent against similar crimes, an appropriate sanction for the commission of certain serious crimes, and a way to maintain public safety.

Opponents believe it fails as a deterrent and is inherently cruel and point to the risk of wrongful conviction. The constitutionality of the juvenile death penalty has been the subject of intense national debate in the last decade. Several Supreme Court decisions and high-profile cases have led to increased public interest and closer examination of the issues by academics, legislators, and policymakers.

The research of Robinson and Stephens applied five descriptive categories to ninety-one juveniles who had been sentenced to death between 1973 and 1991. The categories were based on mitigating circumstances that had been established by the evidence and were in addition to "youth" as a mitigating factor as established in *Eddings v. Oklahoma*. Robinson found that:

1. Almost half of those sentenced had troubled family histories and social backgrounds and problems such as physical abuse, unstable childhood environments, and illiteracy.
2. Twenty-nine suffered psychological disturbances (e.g., profound depression, paranoia, and self-mutilation).
3. Just under one-third exhibited mental disability evidenced by low or borderline IQ scores.
4. More than half were indigent.
5. Eighteen were involved in intensive substance abuse before the crime.

Juveniles sentenced to death share varying combinations of these mitigating circumstances, in addition to their youthful age. "In 61 of the 91 cases (67 percent), one or more factors in addition to 'youth' were present."

Individuals who were juveniles at the time they committed a capital offense continue to be sentenced to the death penalty in the United States. Although the number of juvenile offenders affected by the death penalty is small, these offenders serve as a focal point for often highly politicized debates about the constitutionality of the death penalty, public safety, alternatives available to judges and juries in determining the fates of these youth, and, most crucial, the effectiveness of the juvenile justice system in safeguarding the due process rights of youth.

YOUTH WITH SPECIAL NEEDS

Youth with special needs, including ethnic minorities, females, mentally retarded, developmentally delayed, medically fragile, and violent adolescents, require unique intervention and treatment services. Specialized and culturally competent interventions must be integrated into the treatment plan of these youth. Collaboration with external and internal care systems and providers is especially important with these adolescents for the purposes of management and aftercare services. Some community programs provide separate housing units for these youth, as they benefit from smaller units, less stimulation, and more individual interaction (Underwood, Mullan, and Walter 1997).

The following adaptations might be considered:

1. Specialized training for all staff working with the group.
2. Additional time with treatment interventions.
3. Repetition of clinically relevant information.
4. Graphic illustrations of program expectations.
5. Use of behavioral rating systems.
6. Modified positive reinforcement schedules (Underwood et al. 2006).

Youth with special needs often do not have the capacity to truly understand the full impact of their actions. Therefore should these youth receive the same kind of consequences or punishments? Recently there have been many cases where special needs youth have received the full extent of the law and have been imprisoned not having a full understanding of the process or the reasons for the imprisonment. The corrections system needs to become much aware of special needs youth and their challenges and begin to be creative in finding differentiated ways of rehabilitation so as to have success.

FACILITY OVERCROWDING

In the review of several government reports the numbers of facilities that are overcrowded are more the norm than the exception. Crowding occurs when the number of residents occupying all or part of a facility exceeds some predetermined limit based on square footage, utility use, or even fire codes. Although not a perfect measure of crowding, comparing the number of residents to the number of standard beds gives a sense of the crowding problem in a facility. Even if a facility is not relying on makeshift beds, e.g., cots, roll-out beds, mattresses, sofas, a facility may be overcrowded. For example, using standard beds in an infirmary for youth who are not sick or beds in seclusion for youth who have not committed infractions may indicate crowding problems.

Overcrowding leads to youth fighting for territory, personal space, and establishment of boundaries. Overcrowding is known for fueling tempers and power struggles and survival of the fittest. There are more injuries when youth are crowded together. If you put too many rats in a cage they kill each other till the equilibrium of the environment is reset.

The goal of the corrections system should be to do a triage of youth offenders and classify them according to a scale that measures, predisposition to violence, mental health, ability to be reformed and students needing medical attention and direct them to the right kind of facility that can meet their needs. This may be only a dream at this time as the corrections system is all about containment and not necessarily rehabilitation.

DEATHS OF JUVENILES IN CUSTODY

This is a very rare phenomenon but does occur occasionally. The number one cause is suicide by the youth. Many youth detention centers do screen youths for predisposition to suicidal risk or tendencies. Youths are interviewed at intake and are often monitored by counseling staff throughout their stay. Many youths have been transported to the hospital for suicide attempts, but very few are successful at accomplishing their goal of killing themselves. Detention centers are very aware of the factors that may cause youths to want to take their lives and have become very proactive about the assessment and monitoring of these youth. At times many of these youths are on a 24/7 watch and therefore are protected by the institution and the staff.

SEXUAL VIOLENCE IN JUVENILE FACILITIES

The Prison Rape Elimination Act of 2003 (PREA) requires the Bureau of Justice Statistics (BJS) to report the incidence and prevalence of sexual violence in adult and juvenile detention and correctional facilities. Sexual violence is divided into:

1. youth-on-youth nonconsensual sexual acts,
2. youth-on-youth abusive sexual contacts,
3. staff-on-youth sexual misconduct, and
4. staff-on-youth sexual harassment that includes verbal harassment (Juvenile Offenders and Victims National Report 2006).

Most of the offenses of sexual offense seem to be between youth on youth, while staff on youth seems to be less but definitely present. The attacks are often not reported because of fear of retaliation or punishment by a staff member. The statistics that are reported are often around the 60 percent mark for youth on youth attacks but officials estimate that these numbers are probably much higher because of the lack of reporting or staff not recognizing the signs that a youth has been attacked physically or sexually. Rape is alive and well in the youth facilities.

The Juvenile Offenders and Victims National Report reported "that 34% of the victims in the substantiated incidents of sexual violence in state-operated facilities were female, although females accounted for just 11% of the custody population. Similarly, although females represented 17% of the population in local or private facilities, 37% of the victims in substantiated incidents of sexual violence in these facilities were female."

"Females were more likely than males to be sexually victimized, males constituted a greater proportion of the victims of substantiated nonconsensual sexual acts between youth (78%)." It seems that incarcerated males are more likely to prey sexually on male youths within their environment.

Males and females were equally likely to be the victims of abusive youth-on youth sexual contact. "In substantiated incidents of staff sexual misconduct females accounted for 32% of the victims. In substantiated incidents of sexual violence, a female (youth or staff) was the perpetrator in 24% of incidents in local or private facilities and 36% of incidents overall." The Juvenile Offenders and Victims National Report found that the allegation rate of youth-on-youth nonconsensual sexual acts reported by authorities in juvenile facilities was more "than 6 times the rate of inmate-on-inmate nonconsensual sexual acts reported by authorities in state prisons and more than 7 times the rate in local jails. Similarly, the rate of staff sexual misconduct was 10 times greater in state-operated juvenile facilities than in state prisons and 5 times greater in local or private juvenile facilities than in local jails."

The national report pointed out that these differences may not reflect actual differences in the levels of sexual violence. For example, "all sexual acts between youth in juvenile facilities were legally classified as nonconsensual, but consensual acts between inmates were not counted in adult facilities," In addition, professionals in many states are required by law to report any suspicion of child abuse, including sexual contacts among juveniles. "Allegations in juvenile facilities were more likely to be investigated by external authorities than those in adult facilities, which might encourage more reporting to juvenile facility authorities."

Finally, the national report found that the records systems in juvenile facilities concluded "sexual violence may be more readily reported to authorities in juvenile facilities than in adult facilities" (Juvenile Victims and Offenders National Report 2006).

YOUTH IN ADULT JAILS

At any given time there is only about 1 percent of the juvenile offender population in adult jails throughout the United States. The Juvenile Justice and Delinquency Prevention Act prevents youths from being jailed with adult prisoners. The act states that "juveniles alleged to be or found to be delinquent," as well as status offenders and nonoffenders, "will not be detained or confined in any institution in which they have contact with adult inmates."

This provision of the act is commonly referred to as the "sight and sound separation requirement." Subsequent regulations implementing the act clarify this requirement and provide that brief and inadvertent contact in nonresidential areas is not a violation. The act also states that "no juvenile shall be detained or confined in any jail or lockup for adults."

This provision is known as the jail and lockup removal requirement. Regulations exempt juveniles being tried as criminals for felonies or who have been convicted as criminal felons from the jail and lockup removal requirement. "In institutions other than adult jails or lockups or in jails and lockups under temporary hold exceptions, confinement of juvenile offenders is permitted if juveniles and adult inmates cannot see each other and no conversation between them is possible." This reflects the sight and sound separation requirement.

Some temporary hold exceptions to jail and lockup removal include: "a 6-hour grace period that allows adult jails and lockups to hold alleged delinquents in secure custody until other arrangements can be made (including 6 hours before and after court appearances) and a 48-hour exception, exclusive of weekends and holidays, for rural facilities that meet statutory conditions."

Some jurisdictions have established juvenile detention centers that are collocated with adult jails or lockups. A collocated juvenile facility must meet specific criteria to establish that it is a separate and distinct facility. The regulations allow time-phased use of program areas in collocated facilities (Juvenile Offenders and Victims National Report 2006).

• • •

In conclusion one must begin to evaluate the whole system of youth corrections. We know that there have been improvements in how services are delivered, monitored, and evaluated for youth in trouble. It is imperative that we begin to meet the needs of youths in all aspects of their development (emotionally, physically, and socially).

Society needs to become more aware of its cultures and values. We need to become more proactive and respond earlier to children exhibiting problem behaviors and not wait till they become a statistic in the system. It is by taking responsibility that we will empower children and youth to be responsible and great citizens instead of being a throwaway by-product of its ineffectiveness. We can begin with one child in one town in one state anywhere.

8

Hate Crimes by Juveniles

This chapter will focus on reporting a variety of hate crimes committed by a child or a youth. The motivation to act out violently has many roots and factors. Those factors could be fueled by genetics, environmental conditions, poor parenting, alcohol and drug abuse, psychological impairment or trauma, mental health illness, or traumatic events such as abuse or neglect in the early years.

Educators, mental health professionals, and law enforcement officials have spent many hours trying to figure out what motivates a child or youth to commit a crime. The puzzle to solving that dilemma is ongoing and as individual as the youth themselves. There are common themes that seem to be consistent in the background of the youth. The lack of connection to people or community is instrumental in acting out.

Many of the crimes have been committed out of a desire for money or drugs. There are incidents that have been based in pure hate because the victim is part of a minority or a marginalized group. There are attacks that have been motivated by the desire to join a gang or to be accepted by a certain group of kids within a school or community.

The formula for this chapter will include the description of the individual committing the crime, the crime itself, the sentence for the crime, and any public or community response if any was noted in the media. Motivation may also be included if known.

CASE 1

Two white females, one black male. Three teens: the girls were seventeen and the boy was eighteen at the time of the attack. One girl was training to be a beauty therapist. The attack took place September 25, 2009 in London's Trafalgar Square. The kids were intoxicated and disorderly.

Description of the crime: A gay man was attacked and died after being subjected to homophobic taunts in Trafalgar Square, the Old Bailey heard today. Ian Baynham, sixty-two, died from a brain injury eighteen days after being punched to the ground on September 25th. He was confronted by two teenage girls outside South Africa House after they had been drinking. Baynham was with his friend Philip Brown and they were called "fucking faggots," it was alleged. "Ian Baynham was openly homosexual. What led to his death began when Ruby Thomas hurled homophobic abuse at him and his friend Philip Brown."

A confrontation between Thomas and the victim escalated when he slapped Burke. Alexander then felled Baynham with such force that he hit the back of his head on the pavement and became unconscious. That did not suffice. There is evidence that the female defendants then began putting the boot into Mr. Baynham, who was still prone on his back, clearly unconscious and in distress. "Shocked onlookers saw repeated stamping to his chest and forceful kicks to his head."

Burke repeatedly punched Brown in the face when he tried to stop her running into an Underground station nearby. One witness also said he saw them pointing at another pair of gay men, walking hand in hand, and one saying, "We can do them," with the other nodding enthusiastically. Others saw them acting aggressively and having to be restrained by their friends when they reached Trafalgar Square at about 10 p.m. The day after the event the girl contacted another friend who was a witness and she asked him what had happened the night before because she couldn't remember.

Before the attack on Mr. Baynham, witnesses described drunken blondes Thomas and Burke swaggering round Trafalgar Square with cans of beer intent on causing trouble. One onlooker likened the level of violence to a scene from the film Clockwork Orange—"a scene of despicable violence." The youths were arrested and jailed. The motivation seemed to be homophobia fueled by drunkenness (Cohen 2010).

CASE 2

Three young women, two young men, twelve- to fifteen-years old, between March 31 and April 2009.

Description of the crime: They typically waited in the lobbies of the apartment complexes. Once they spotted a target, they would surround the victims. The young women would beat them with their hands and fists while the young men watch. Bizarre facts: No money was taken in the attacks, and the victims had no prior contact with their attackers, according to investigators. These youths seem to randomly pick certain women because they were Asian. The motivation seemed based in racism. They were detained and became part of the Juvenile Detention system. Sentence was not published because of age of individuals (wn.com/Police_Assault_17-Year-Old_Kid_in_Brooklyn,_NY).

CASE 3

A thirteen-year-old boy in eighth grade, Cherry Creek, Colorado.

Description of the crime: This youth beat up student Adrian Ulm at the bus stop while a group of a dozen students watched. Adrian was bullied and harassed because he was German. The student would call him a "Nazi" and "gay" because of his heritage and because he liked theater. The attacker broke his collar bone and gave him a head injury.

Sentence: There was no sentence because they both agreed to fight; however, the attacker could be held responsible if a two-year-old amendment to Colorado's hate-crime laws could make Adrian's assailant the first youth in Colorado to be sued for punitive damages on the basis of school bullying. A clear case of harassment and bullying based on student being of another ethnic group (www.denverpost.com/commented/ci_8299250).

CASE 4

Jordan Brown, eleven years old, February 2009.

Description of the crime: Brown shot his stepmom who was eight months pregnant. He shot her in the head and then boarded the bus for school. Sentence: Still waiting trial, will be tried as an adult, if convicted he will be one of the youngest children to receive a life sentence. Family said that the youth had talked about wanting to pop his stepmother in the head. The motivation was jealousy as he did not want to have a sibling (www.prodeathpenalty.com/repeat_murder.htm).

CASE 5

A seventeen-year-old white male, Fenton, Missouri, was physically and mentally abused as a child and was addicted to drugs and alcohol. Subsequent to his sentence of death, clinical psychologist Robert L. Smith evaluated

Christopher. Dr. Smith found that Christopher "was the victim of a dysfunctional home environment . . . , had a self-absorbed and helpless mother . . . and
had no loving and supportive male role-model . . . (his natural father being
distant and critical, his stepfather being inconsistent and emotionally and
physically abusive)." He concluded that Christopher had a "longstanding history of abusing alcohol and marijuana, beginning at age 13 . . . and suffered
from a schizotypal personality disorder."

Description of the crime: Simmons and Benjamin entered the home of the
victim, Shirley Crook, after reaching through an open window and unlocking
the back door. Simmons turned on a hallway light. Awakened, Mrs. Crook
called out, "Who's there?" In response Simmons entered Mrs. Crook's bedroom, where he recognized her from a previous car accident involving them
both. Simmons later admitted this confirmed his resolve to murder her.

Using duct tape to cover her eyes and mouth and bind her hands, the two
perpetrators put Mrs. Crook in her minivan and drove to a state park. They
reinforced the bindings, covered her head with a towel, and walked her to a
railroad trestle spanning the Meramec River. There they tied her hands and
feet together with electrical wire, wrapped her whole face in duct tape, and
threw her from the bridge, drowning her in the waters below.

Sentence: The state charged Simmons with burglary, kidnapping, stealing,
and murder in the first degree. He was initially sentenced to the death penalty,
but because he was seventeen when he committed the crime they reversed it
to just life in prison without probation or parole. He and a sixteen-year-old
friend had been under the influence of convicted felon Brian Moomey, who
regularly had teens commit crimes and bring the proceeds back to him. Motivation: Simmons was bragging about the killing, telling friends he had killed
a woman "because the bitch seen my face." There is little doubt that Simmons
was the instigator of the crime.

Before its commission Simmons said he wanted to murder someone. In
chilling, callous terms he talked about his plan, discussing it for the most part
with two friends, Charles Benjamin and John Tessmer, then aged fifteen and
sixteen respectively. Simmons proposed to commit burglary and murder by
breaking and entering, tying up a victim, and throwing the victim off a bridge.
Simmons assured his friends they could "get away with it" because they were
minors (www.law.cornell.edu/supct/html/03-633.ZO.html).

CASE 6

Edlington, South Yorkshire, twelve- and ten-year-old boys, brothers who
were living in foster care, April, 2009.

Description of the crime: During a sustained and sadistic attack on April 4, they repeatedly threatened to kill the boys, aged just nine and eleven, and forced them to perform a sex act together. At one point a disused kitchen sink was dropped on the head of the older boy and a noose put around his neck. He was then thrown thirty feet into a disused railway line and left, half naked, drifting in and out of consciousness face down in the mud. The younger victim was burned with cigarette ends on his eyelids and ear before being stabbed with a sharpened stick and cigarettes were pushed into his open wounds.

Sentence: sentenced to five years and then will be reevaluated to determine if they are a threat to society. Bizarre facts: The victims were stripped of their underwear and the brothers even filmed their vicious attack on two young boys. The elder brother also viewed his father's porn and horror films, drank vodka and cider, smoked ten cigarettes a day, and used marijuana grown by his father. People's response to the juvenile's behavior (parents-friends-teachers, etc.): "They're animals, absolute animals. How any child could do this to another child I don't know." "The bottom line for the two of you is that I'm sure you both pose a very high risk of serious harm to others." "Your crimes are truly exceptional."

Motivation: They had nothing else to do and so were bored and decided to do this horrific attack (www.telegraph.co.uk/.../crime/.../Schoolboys -plead-guilty-to-torture-attack).

CASE 7

Oxnard, California, E. O. Green Junior High School, fourteen-year-old male, Brandon McInerney. February 12, 2008.

Description of the crime: On the morning of Feb. 12, Lawrence was in the school's computer lab with twenty-four other students, said Mr. Keith, the police spokesman. Brandon walked into the room with a gun and shot Lawrence in the head, the police said, then ran from the building. Police officers caught him a few blocks away. Unconscious when he arrived at the hospital, Lawrence was declared brain dead the next day but kept on a ventilator to preserve his organs for donation, said the Ventura County medical examiner, Armando Chavez.

He was taken off life support on Feb. 14. Lawrence King was an openly gay student. He was adopted when he was a toddler and then placed in a group home and treatment center after being placed on probation for theft and vandalism and claiming that his adopted father abused him.

Brandon McInerney came from a family with a history of crime and violence. His mother was addicted to methamphetamines and his father shot his mom in the arm once, and strangled her to unconsciousness another time. Brandon tried to get other kids to join in on the assault on King. None of his friend would join in, so he did it himself. The day before the shooting, McInerney, who had experience target shooting with the gun used in the crime, told one of King's friends, "Say goodbye to your friend Larry because you're never going to see him again."

Sentence: The district attorney chose to charge Brandon with one count of murder and two enhancements, use of a gun and hate crime; he was tried as an adult and faces fifty-three years in prison without parole.

Bizarre facts: King had apparently become attracted to McInerney leading up to the shooting and this lead to McInerney to be picked on as well. People were teasing him saying he was gay because he was getting upset about being picked on.

People's response to the juvenile's behavior (parents-friends-teachers, etc.): "As the suspect's name passed from cell phone to cell phone, disbelief set in. Not Brandon McInerney, his friends said, "No way." Brandon, fourteen, a tall, athletic eighth-grader, was described by friends and acquaintances as a mellow, focused kid, but one who wouldn't back down in a confrontation.

In the days before the shooting, Brandon had been heard telling Larry to leave him alone, that he would hurt him. Something was building, friends said. Brandon joined the Young Marine Corps' equivalent of a JROTC program several years ago and became a leader in the group, which disbanded in 2008. Brandon was a young man that I never would have figured being involved in something like this, said Mel Otte, his commanding officer. Otte said he never witnessed Brandon showing a short temper and that he would have been kicked out of the group if he had bullied others. He was an outstanding young man, Otte said. What happened since I left, I have no idea. Brandon was tall for his age, and his hours in a martial arts studio helped trim his physique into a lean, muscular one.

Motivation: King had started hitting on Brandon. It was believed that he had an attraction to him. Brandon was being made fun of a lot for it. Was afraid people would think he was gay (www.nytimes.com/2008/02/23/us/23oxnard.html).

CASE 8

Dominique Vallier, seventeen-year-old black male, Baton Rouge, Louisiana, throughout Mardi Gras, February 23, 2009.

Description of the crime: Hispanic man was shot in the leg after he attempted to stop two men from robbing his brother. Dominique shot a Hispanic man in the chest as retaliation, even though this man was not involved in the first incident. Dominique was an accomplice to his friend Anthony Michael Hatcher. These were hate crimes because they targeted Latinos.

On Feb. 24, the men allegedly shot 35-year-old Raymond Caraballo multiple times during an apparent robbery attempt at Academy and Barrow streets in Houma, police said. Minutes later, the men shot another man at Church and School streets, police said. Caraballo was taken to Terrebonne General Medical Center for surgery but died from his injuries, police said. The other shooting victim survived.

Sentence: charged with attempted armed robbery, attempted first-degree murder, and hate crimes because the victims were specifically targeted because of their Hispanic ethnicity (www.trendsinhate.com/hatedates/February-HateDates/February23.html).

CASE 9

August 2003, Gary Hirte, seventeen-year-old, straight-A high school student, Eagle Scout, track football and wrestling star. Weyauwega, Wisconsin.

Description of the crime: Hirte said, when he drank, he sometimes had homosexual urges. He said Kopitske pulled up in his car that night and flirted with him, and they agreed to go back to the older man's house. "We both knew when he offered to go to his house that's what we were gonna do. Something . . . homosexual," Hirte said. Hirte said he had never been with a man before and that their encounter was consensual. But Hirte also says, after the alleged sexual encounter, he went back to his car, fell asleep for a while, and woke up sober and in a rage about having had sex with another man.

He said he went back to Kopitske's house later that night. "I saw myself just command him to lie down on the floor, and from there, I saw myself shoot him, I saw myself stab him twice," he said. "The second stab actually got stuck in his spine. And just in this state of rage, I picked his whole body up with my one arm to get the knife out," he said. He used a shotgun and a hunting knife.

Sentence: Mandatory life in prison, but may be eligible for parole in thirty-two years.

Bizarre facts: Had a homosexual encounter with the man before he shot the man. "There's no reason I should be held accountable for this. That's just the way I feel. I can't change that," Gary Hirte told ABC News' Cynthia McFadden. "It wasn't this mind that's thinking right now that did that action. So I can't feel guilty for it," he said. Before the crime he was getting drunk while listening to Nirvana. He allegedly consumed six bottles of malt liquor and fifteen shots of vodka. Hirte said he believed a homosexual act was not as bad as "raping somebody or torturing somebody" but was worse than murder. Friends said he liked to kill animals with his car. He believed he was doing the man a favor by killing him.

People's response to the juvenile's behavior (parents-friends-teachers etc): "I really believe in my heart that Gary Hirte had seemingly accomplished everything and he thought he would do the most outrageous [thing], the event that would really make people go 'Wow, I don't believe it,'" said Winnebago County District Attorney Bill Lennon.

Motivation: Authorities called it a cold-blooded thrill killing. Hirte claimed initially that it was intentional homicide, but then later claimed that he went temporarily insane, in a murderous rage in which he didn't know right from wrong because of their homosexual encounter. A friend said that Hirte claimed that he felt he was superior to other people and he just wanted to see if he could get away with it (abcnews.go.com).

CASE 10

Steven T. Hollis, eighteen, and Juan L. Flythe, seventeen, Baltimore, Maryland, black males, members of a subset group of the gang the Bloods. They are known as the family swans.

Description of the crime: stabbed and stomped to death, after the two found what they thought to be gay text messages on the victim's cell phone. They walked the victim out into the woods. An autopsy revealed that the victim died of both blunt-force and stabbing injuries, according to court records. He suffered fifty superficial cutting wounds to his arms, neck, head, wrist, and hands in addition to one stab wound to the chest that injured his heart and caused significant blood loss. He also had bruises on the left side of his neck.

Sentence: First degree murder. They were held without bail.

Bizarre facts: Police say fellow gang members discovered that the victim had sent a suggestive text message to another male, along with a photo of his private parts. Court documents say the leaders didn't want to "appear weak to other Blood gang sets if it was revealed that they had a gang member who was gay." The victim's pants were removed.

People's response to the juvenile's behavior (parents-friends-teachers, etc.): "It's awful," Baltimore County prosecutor William B. Bickel said in an interview after the bail-review hearing. "You're talking about a gangland-style execution because he was gay. They took him out back in a field and stabbed him to death." The victim's next door neighbor says she thought the victim was a nice kid.

Motivation: They were afraid their gang would look weak if word got out that they had a gay member in it (www.queerty.com/bloods-members-murdered-gay-mate-say-baltimore-police -20080819/).

CASE 11

Dustin Lynch, fifteen-year-old white male, runaway, Medina, Ohio. November 2, 2002.

Description of the crime: Stabbed the female victim on the side after bashing her with a bedpost. He then covered her with a pile of clothes. He had been staying with them for about a week when the event occurred. It sparked a big controversy in the video game world because people blamed the game Grand Theft Auto III for the attack. During his week stay he supposedly played the game for hours on end.

Bizarre facts: Lynch, seventeen, claims to have begun thinking about murder at an early age: "Ever since I was 6 years old, I've wanted to kill someone," he wrote. The teen claims to have killed thirty-five people, though there is no evidence backing up his assertion. "The only people I care about are Adolf Hitler and myself! Heil the fuehrer! Hitler is God!" he wrote to the paper. The young man says he's not afraid of prison, hoping to get his high-school diploma and write a book while there. "I might be small, but I know how to handle my business," he writes. "I'm a 'Lynch,' it runs through [our] blood. Just like jail!" Lynch claims he'd like to be executed eventually. "When my book is complete and I'm ready, I'm going to kill someone else so that I can get the death penalty. I took so many lives and I'm just curious to know what it's like to be dead. Is there an after life? I want to die by lethal injection. I think that is better than any other method (ex. - killing myself, or by some horrible death)." Asked if he was disturbed, Lynch wrote to the *Scene*: "I AM NOT DISTURBED AT ALL! Like I said, I have certain needs, desires and a fetish. Cutting myself is a fetish. I feel so powerful when I do it, kind of like I'm on coke. Each slice I take is like hooting another line! I'm fascinated by the sight of blood, and when I'm locked up the way I am the only blood I can get is my own."

People's response to the juvenile's behavior (parents-friends-teachers, etc): JoLynn Mishne's father believed he was influenced by the game Grand Theft Auto. Mr. Mishne claimed that Dustin would play the game for hours at a time.

Motivation: When asked why he killed JoLynn, Lynch responded, "I killed JoLynn for my own personal satisfaction. I yearn to see blood; it's a need or an addiction and also a fetish. I'm just obsessed with it all." "I killed JoLynn

Mishne for my own personal satisfaction, not because of a video game," adding that he "did her a favor and satisfied all my needs while doing it!"

Sentence: He was sentenced to thirty years in jail (www.corsinet.com/trivia/texts/121203favor.txt).

CASE 12

Woburn Massachusetts, fifteen-year-old white male, John Odgren, attending Lincoln Sudbury Regional High School, Jan. 19, 2007. John has depression and Asperger's Syndrome ADHD and was possibly bipolar.

Description of the crime: Stabbed a young man in the stall of a bathroom at his high school. Brought a carving knife to school, picked a random person, and stabbed him eight times. He attacked a freshman whom he's never met. He planned his crime, executed it, and showed extreme cruelty. He showed many signs that he could potentially be violent.

Sentence: guilty of first degree murder and life in prison.

Bizarre facts: He often talked of committing the perfect murder. Odgren became obsessed with Stephen King novels, violence, crime, and forensics. He also developed an "irrational fear that something was going to happen to him. He started bringing weapons to school, once a knife and another time a toy gun." By January 2009, Odgren was "consumed by his delusions."

People's response to the juvenile's behavior (parents-friends-teachers, etc.): Why did a geeky, uncoordinated, awkward 16-year-old who had never been in any trouble with the law suddenly and without provocation ferociously stab to death a 15-year-old classmate who he did not even know? Odgren was on at least three psychotropic drugs, and has been weeping and stunned by the result. He said he had been comforted by a stuffed bunny, which he was allowed to embrace during breaks in the trial.

Motivation: The randomness of the attack may indicate a psychological breakdown due to his disability; however, no concrete explanation exists for the bizarre behavior (insession.blogs.cnn.com/.../medical-experts-odgren -had-obsession-with-the-dark-tower-novel-series/).

CASE 13

Evan Savoie and Jake Eakin, February 15, 2003, Ephrata, Washington. The two young white males committed a crime. Eakin has learning disabilities and a low IQ.

Description of the crime: Craig Sorger, thirteen, was found beaten and stabbed thirty-four times in an Ephrata recreational vehicle park. He was wearing handcuffs, eyeglasses, and slicked-back, shoulder-length hair. A pale Eakin trembled at times as he described from the witness stand the rainy day he and Savoie went to the park to play. At one point, Savoie pulled a knife out of his pocket and told Eakin he "wanted to go on a killing spree."

Minutes later, the boys went to Sorger's nearby travel trailer, where his family was living, to ask him to play. Eakin said they roamed the park, playing near a canal, for several minutes before stopping to build a fort in a wooded area. Savoie then asked Sorger to feel the ground to see if it was wet. He told Sorger to touch the ground for ten seconds; Sorger got on his knees and began counting to ten. At nine, Savoie dropped a rock the "size of a basketball" on the back of Sorger's neck, knocking the boy to the ground, Eakin said. Eakin paused as he recalled the look of pain on Sorger's face, taking his only long look at Savoie.

"I got up and tried to stop him. I just told him, I just got up and I was like, 'Stop,'" Eakin said. "He pushed me." Savoie then began hitting Sorger—perhaps more than thirty times, Eakin said. Several times Sorger tried to get away, crying out, "Why are you doing this to me?" but Savoie repeatedly pulled him back to the ground and continued striking him. Eakin said he didn't see anything in Savoie's hand, but did see blood coming from Savoie's neck as the boy cried out.

"He was saying that he was dying," Eakin said. "He was face down. Evan was on top on his knees." The attack lasted just minutes, after which Sorger remained motionless on the ground, Eakin said. Looking down at his hands on his lap, and flushing slightly, Eakin then recounted how he picked up a stick and began hitting Sorger in the head and legs more than twenty times before throwing the stick to the ground. Savoie said nothing, Eakin said. "He walked to me and he shook my hand."

Sentence: Eakin got a 14-year sentence, Savoie life in prison.

People's response to the juvenile's behavior (parents-friends-teachers, etc.): Evan was the class clown and popular at school. He was the one who met Craig first and introduced him to Jake, even though they had only played together a few times. By most accounts, Evan was the leader in their friendship. "[Jake's] not really [my] best friend. I think one step lower. I call him my step-friend," explains Evan. "I don't know why, I just made up the name step-friend. So that's what I call him." His mother, Tammy Vickery, says if he were guilty, there would have been more blood: "If somebody's been stabbed 34 times, and then beat with a stick 16 times, you're going to have more than one speck of blood on you. . . . Deep down in my heart, my son, I know he's innocent."

"They look like little boys, they act like little boys. They're actually described as being nice, polite. Kids that have friends that, like other people, that relate well to their families," says Johnson. Motivation: Brutality for the sake of brutality. Motivation was to be powerful and in charge (www.spokesmanreview.com/breaking/story.asp?ID=6486).

CASE 14

May 30, 2003, Fishtown, Philadelphia. Justina Morely, fifteen-year-old white female, Nicholas Coia, sixteen, his brother Dominec Coia, seventeen, and the victim's best friend Edward Batzig, sixteen.

Description of the crime: Morley, meanwhile, met Sweeney and started walking him to "the trails"—an overgrown and desolate industrial wasteland off Beach Street—a popular spot for local teens to hang out and party. For some unknown reason, sources said the couple failed to rendezvous with the killers, prompting an angry call from the boys to Morley's cell phone.

Morley, according to law enforcement sources, shot right back at her co-conspirators. "What did you do, bitch out?" she allegedly asked. The parties agreed to return to the trails. This time, police said, Morley delivered her suitor to the slaughter. They walked down a black gravel road toward a junction of trees. Morley began to undress. Then Sweeney took off his shoes. That's as far as he got.

A blow came from a small-handled hatchet. It struck Sweeney on the head and knocked him to the ground. Sources said it was followed by blows from a hammer and more blows from the hatchet as he tried to get up. Another assailant used a brick. Later, one of the boys used what one detective described as a "boulder" type of rock to crush Sweeney's head. Nearly all of the blows struck Sweeney on the head and face, according to a source familiar with the injuries. As the grisly slaying unfolded, Morley stood off to the side and did not take part, according to sources.

When it was over, though, she allegedly shared in the blood money —$500—divided four ways, or a total of $125 apiece, for murder. "The motive was robbery," said Sergeant Kathleen McGowan of the homicide division. "They planned to rob him and use the money to get high." Sweeney's head and face were so badly beaten that his body was nearly unidentifiable.

Sentence: life in prison without the possibility of parole.

Bizarre facts: Listened to the Beatles "Helter Skelter" over and over again. The song was made famous by the serial killer Charles Manson. The kids showed little remorse, during the arrest they asked "When are we going home?" Four teenagers planned the killing for weeks, listened repeatedly on the day to the song linked to mass murderer Charles Manson, and then came together for a "group hug" after they beat sixteen-year-old Jason Sweeney to death in a vacant Fishtown lot, according to alleged confessions from two of them. Batzig, once Sweeney's best friend, told investigators: "We just walked up and started hitting him. . . . Soon after that, Jason started begging for his life." She cried on the stand, but Morley was acting a part. "I'm a cold-blooded death-worshiping bitch who survives by feeding off the weak and lonely. I lure them, and then I crush them," Morley wrote last year. "I am guilty. But I still don't feel guilty for anything. . . . I still enjoy my flashbacks. They give me comfort. I love them."

On the stand, Morley acknowledged that, before Sweeney was slain, she had sex with both Nicholas Coia and Batzig in exchange for heroin. And shortly after they were arrested, she stripped for the trio in a prison van on the way to the courthouse.

People's response to the juvenile's behavior (parents-friends-teachers, etc): "One of the most disturbing jobs I've ever seen. That kid is lying on a slab in a morgue still screaming in pain."

Many in the neighborhood said Dominic and Nicholas Coia, who had moved into the area only a couple of years earlier, were known as bad news. According to Keith Hunter, twenty-nine, "They robbed cars, broke windows." By contrast, friends of Morley, a pretty, dark-haired girl who liked punk music, said they were shocked to hear of her alleged involvement in the crime.

Motivation: To steal money and spend it on drugs. Sweeney said she felt the killing was about thrills, rather than money (www.findadeath.com).

CASE 15

June 25, 2003, sixteen- and fourteen-year-old Josh and William Buckner, Newport, Tennessee. Will was born with mild brain damage, IQ of 91. Josh's mom died when he was seven. Josh has ADHD.

Description of the crime: Both shot bullets onto the highway from the woods near their home. Killed one person and wounded another.

Sentence: Will and Josh pleaded guilty to reckless homicide, reckless endangerment, and aggravated assault and were sentenced to a nearby juvenile detention center, where they live today. According to state law, they can be detained only until the age of nineteen.

Bizarre facts: Stepbrothers who bonded because they both could relate to coming from unstable families. Didn't mean to hurt anyone; they wanted to shoot at the sides of trucks after playing Grand Theft Auto III. They had a history of playing with guns. The father would take them out in the woods shooting with him, and one day a week or so before the shooting the boys were found cleaning off a .22. The night of the crime they snuck into the parents' room, while the parents were home and stole the guns; then they lied and said they were going out for a ride on the 4-wheeler.

People's response to the juveniles' behavior (parents-friends-teachers, etc.): "What's intriguing about this case is that there was a lack of a motive," says Jack Thompson, the lawyer who launched the suit. "They were acting out the game." And, today, the stepbrothers' friends, family, and even the Buckner boys themselves suggest that it was much more than a video game that sent the bullets flying from nowhere that night. "They aren't serial killers. They're good boys." Josh was warm with friends and family, giving big and frequent hugs. Popular with the girls, he was the only boy invited to his friend Sara Sample's slumber party. "He was like a little puppy dog," Sara's mother, Mandy Epley, recalled. Motivation: Wanted to act out a video game (www.salon.com/technology/feature/2005/02/22/gta_killers).

CASE 16

Three-month crime spree in the Washington, D.C. area, by Lee Boyd Malvo, a seventeen-year-old black male, born in Kingston, Jamaica.

Description of the crime: Sniper who shot thirteen people and killed ten people, with John Allen Muhammed. Lee Malvo as part of his testimony outlined Muhammad's complete, multiphase plan. His plan consisted of three phases in the Washington, D.C. and Baltimore metro areas. Phase one consisted of meticulously planning, mapping, and practicing their locations around the D.C. area. This way after each shooting they would be able to quickly leave the area on a predetermined path, and move on to the next location. Muhammad's goal in phase one was to kill six white people a day for thirty days. Malvo went on to describe how phase one did not go as planned due to heavy traffic and the lack of a clear shot and/or getaway at different locations. Phase two was meant to be moved up to Baltimore. Malvo described how this phase was close to being implemented, but never was carried out.

Phase two was intended to begin by killing a pregnant woman by shooting her in the stomach. The next step would have been to shoot and kill a Baltimore police officer. At the officer's funeral, there were to be created several improvised explosive devices. These explosives were intended to kill a large number of police, since many police would attend another officer's funeral.

The last phase was to take place very shortly after, if not during, phase two. The third phase was to extort several million dollars from the U.S. government. This money would be used to finance a larger plan: to travel north into Canada and recruit other effectively orphaned boys to use weapons and stealth, and send them out to commit shootings across the country.

Sentence: Life without the possibility of parole. They toggled with the death sentence, but because he was a minor at the time of the crime they decided against it.

Bizarre facts: Malvo didn't exist on paper in his new American home. He and his mother had been smuggled from St. Elizabeth, Jamaica, to Haiti and then onto a tugboat into Miami, where they illegally entered the United States, according to accounts they gave to immigration officials.

Motivation: It is reported to have been thrill seeking and a sense of power (en.wikipedia.org/wiki/John_Allen_Muhammad).

• • •

These sixteen cases are only a very small list of juvenile crimes. There are thousands in the law books and some occurring every day. These were chosen because they can highlight several themes. Homophobia, thrill seeking, revenge, power, robbery, and just because "I can attitude"; personality dysfunction, mental health and illness are all running themes in these scenarios.

Homophobia is alive and well in America. Being perceived as gay if you are a teenager is a fate worse than death. Many of our young gay people are not safe in our public schools. They become the targets of their peers. Bullying incidents are on the rise. What can be done to teach tolerance and acceptance for teenagers? We need to help young people understand that being different because of sexual orientation is not evil or bad but can be good and positive. America has a long way to go in terms of a society to accept and protect gay teenagers.

Thrill seeking speaks volumes as to what ends a youth will go to ward off boredom. The thought of hurting or killing someone else just to see what happens is disturbing. Youths need to be involved in activities that take them away from sitting in front of a television screen or computer video game and gets them involved with others in the great outdoors or in the community.

We cannot allow youths to isolate themselves in their rooms and lose touch with the reality of interpersonal relationships. We have to force them to interact in whatever ways are appropriate. They have to be exposed to a variety of activities and interests and be able to cultivate those interests in a way that will continue to build social skills and interactions.

Revenge is a human emotion based on some level of perspective of injustice. Youths who seek out revenge often do so as a way to make things equal or to solve their problems. Many of them do not have the ability to communicate effectively through dialogue and interpersonal relationships. Revenge is an easy way to equal the score.

They rarely think through the process of their actions. It is about getting instant gratification and knowing that a wrong whether real or perceived will be accomplished. Youths need to be taught how to problem solve and to communicate rather than lash out in anger. The teaching of these skills needs to begin early and be modeled effectively throughout the early years of school and personality development.

Power is a powerful emotion. The feeling of being all powerful to decide whether another person lives or dies can be intoxicating. The knowledge of being able to dictate the route of another's person destiny can lead an individual to act out. Many youths who have been put in a position of helplessness believe the only way to regain power is to assert themselves.

This assertive behavior often is confused with violence and murder. These youths do not seem to know how to define the clear lines of assertion and aggression. Specific lessons on problem solving and assertion need to be paired together so that an individual can have a list of options when trying to solve issues with another person.

Power is so common in our society that we see it every day if we watch the 6 o'clock news. America's foundation is based on power. There will need to be a redefining of what a culture of peace is really all about both in our homes and communities and our country.

Crimes of robbery against individuals and property are very common in America. As long as we are going to having injustice, inequality, low social economic communities and individual we will have crime. People who do not have material things or sometimes the basic necessities of life want them. Survival for some leads to crime.

However, the majority of youths want what others more privileged have. They see the good life and they want a piece of it. Unfortunately many youths do not have the education or the opportunity to attain this level of comfort due to many environmental conditions or factors in their lives. Youths from minority communities must be given access to education and entrepreneurship so that they have a chance at being successful. There has to be a change in American society from a privileged few to the masses being able to be successful and privileged as well.

The number of youths and children experiencing mental health, personality disorders, and mental illness is staggering in America. Many of these children live in poverty, single parent homes, abusive homes, or foster or group homes or are detained in juvenile detention centers or just roaming the streets. Many schools are the first identifiers of mental illness in children because of their odd behaviors; however very few schools or educators are equipped to handle the issues or to provide services in a timely way.

The state of mental health services in America is pathetic. Many youths do not have access to services because their parents do not have health insurance. Universal health care should begin to address minimally this issue. However, it is still an issue of money, access to services for those in rural areas, and the amount of available professionals. If we continue to not service these young people as they are developing into adolescence and adulthood the more crimes as listed above will continue.

We cannot continue to ignore the fact that children and youth are damaged and dysfunctional. Locking up everyone with mental illness is not an option. We need to develop better screening and assessment tools to identify early on when a child is experiencing mental health concerns. We cannot just hope that it will go away. It often does not and in fact becomes worse with the onset of adolescence.

In conclusion, this chapter was included as a reality check for the reader as to what youths are capable of when they are dysfunctional. The important thing to remember is that we have created these youths through our inability to parent, supervise, educate, and guide. Somewhere along the way these troubled youths became transformed into monsters.

We as a society are guilty of creating them. We can be shocked and bury our heads in the sand and not face the reality that there will be more of these incidents, or we can become proactive as individuals and as a society to start changing how we behave. We can make a difference by our examples.

9

Alternative Programs and Strategies for Children and Youths

Children come in all shapes and sizes. They have different genetics, life and school experiences. They are abused, neglected, mentally ill, psycho-pathetic, and sociopathic as well as having many other clinical diagnoses. Is there a program or a strategy that will work best for these damaged youths? The goal of this chapter is to provide the reader with multiple possibilities that will meet the needs of the children as well as the need of the school, community or home of the troubled youth and children.

"Preventing delinquency," says Peter Greenwood, "not only saves young lives from being wasted, but also prevents the onset of adult criminal careers and thus reduces the burden of crime on its victims and on society." He goes on to say that, "it costs states billions of dollars a year to arrest, prosecute, incarcerate, and treat juvenile offenders. Investing in successful delinquency-prevention programs can save taxpayers seven to ten dollars for every dollar invested, primarily in the form of reduced spending on prisons" (Greenwood).

His reporting of these statistics indicates a real need for states and federal agencies to really begin looking at what works and what is preventative in terms of keeping kids in schools, off the streets, out of crime and violence and becoming productive members of society.

The Annie Casey Foundation has been a leader in juvenile reform and has come up with eight core components that a program must have to actually initiate change. The Foundation has given permission for these eight core components to be reproduced for the discussion in this text.

1. *Collaboration* between the major juvenile justice agencies, other governmental entities, and community organizations. Without collaboration, even well-designed reforms are likely to flounder or be

subverted. A formal structure within which to undertake joint planning and policymaking is essential.

2. It is impossible for agencies to act in isolation of one another. Resources cannot be taken out of one hand to be given to the other. Politicians in Washington and at the state level must have a common goal and want to solve the problem. Not playing together will only create a variety of tunnels that lead to nowhere. Everyone needs to be committed to serving the needs of this population.

3. Use of accurate data, both to diagnose the system's problems and proclivities and to assess the impact of various reforms, is critical.

4. In 2011 it is imperative that all agencies make data driven decisions. It is irresponsible to make decisions that are not well grounded in research or data collection. What the statistics are saying usually indicate the pulse of the problem. Money and resources need to be allocated according to need and demand. States that show a larger need based on very stable statistics should get additional funding and resources to address these issues.

5. Objective admissions criteria and instruments must be developed to replace subjective decision making at all points where choices to place children in secure custody are made.

6. Anytime a child enters the system the evaluation measures that are used for placement or intervention must be based in credible and reliable standards. There needs to be some level of consistency of application and interpretation of the results. It cannot be at the whims of a social worker or a case manager. The decisions made must be based in accurate information gathering and data that supports the hypothesis and the needs.

7. *New or enhanced nonsecure alternatives to detention* must be implemented in order to increase the options available for arrested youth. These programs must be careful to target youth who would otherwise be locked up. Whenever possible, they should be based in neighborhoods where detention cases are concentrated and operated by local organizations.

8. Jail or detention centers are not always the best place for troubled youth yet more often than not that is where they end up. There needs to be a better triage process that evaluates the potential or risk of a youth becoming an aggressor or a victim in the detention system. Often times putting a vulnerable youth in jail only increases the possibility that they will become hardened and even more aggressive.

9. *Case processing reforms* must be introduced to expedite the flow of cases through the system. These changes reduce lengths of stay in

custody, expand the availability of nonsecure program slots, and ensure that interventions with youth are timely and appropriate.

10. The backlog in the American youth justice system is atrocious and pitiful. The amount of young people waiting to be arraigned is obscene in many large cities. There are too many clients and not enough courtrooms. A system of triage in the justice system would alleviate this problem and the courts would be freed up to deal with the very serious cases. A complete overhaul needs to be done to move this process forward. Unfortunately this author is not too optimistic at this time as juvenile justice is very rooted in its old practices and procedures.

11. *Special detention cases*—for youth in custody as a result of probation violations, writs and warrants, as well as those awaiting placement— must be re-examined and new practices implemented to minimize their presence in the secure facility.

12. As mentioned in the above paragraph the juvenile justice system needs to become more efficient in handling and processing the cases before the courts. Holding youths in adult jails has been proven to be ineffective and downright dangerous. Many of the youths who are incarcerated become victims of violence. The appropriateness of these types of placements for youths needs to be well defined and consistently implemented.

13. *Reducing racial disparities* requires specific strategies (in addition to those listed above) aimed at eliminating bias and ensuring a level playing field for youth of color. Change in this arena also requires persistent, determined leadership because the sensitive nature of these discussions and changes frequently provoke defensiveness and avoidance.

14. Youths who are culturally different or part of a minority ethnic group need to be given the right opportunities to succeed like everyone else in America. They need to believe that they are on the same playing field as their Caucasian friends. Discrimination and prejudice in this country has to give way to opportunity for all. Education needs to be of high quality and available. Youth of color need to have a semblance of hope for the future.

15. *Improving conditions of confinement* is most likely to occur when facilities are routinely inspected by knowledgeable individuals applying rigorous protocols and ambitious standards. Absent of this kind of consistent scrutiny, conditions in secure facilities are unlikely to improve and often will deteriorate.

16. We cannot for one moment become complacent about the facilities that house our youth. We need to make them places of rehabilitation

and change. We must continue to regulate the administration of these facilities so that they are places of humanity and dignity and not places of oppression.

It is important to realize that these core initiatives can only happen if communities make the investment into change. To affect the crime rates, the amount of incarcerations systems must be changed. People in power will need to alter their beliefs and attitudes.

RESTORATIVE JUSTICE

A model that has gained favor in both criminal justice and educational system is restorative justice. Restorative justice has roots in tribal cultures throughout the world. Pam Stenhjem has stated that "these cultures have long understood that the needs of both the victim and community must be considered and addressed before amends can be made." In her work around restorative justice she emphasizes one basic concept: crime damages people, communities, and relationships.

This model holds that justice should focus on trying to repair any injustices or damages done to an individual person, or to a community. The process of healing can only be accomplished once all parties have begun to build a sense of trust and have a motivation to resolve the issues. In a way the parties must be prepared to make amends for their actions.

Restorative justice is built upon a community which has a set of standards that are enforceable and can be addressed in the process. The method by which restorative justice is done can include: victim-offender mediation, various community decision-making processes that may include appearance in front of panels, restorative community service (picking up trash, helping the disadvantage, restitution in the form of financial compensation, victim and community impact statements, and victim awareness panels (Stenhjem 2005).

Restorative justice redefines the way justice systems addresses the criminal activity or an offense toward someone else. It provides a forum to make people accountable for their actions. It also empowers people to do the right thing to make things good again.

Umbreit (2000) lists specific examples of restorative justice. The following can be used as part of any restorative program:

1. crime repair crews,
2. victim intervention programs,

3. family group conferencing,
4. victim-offender mediation and dialogue,
5. peacemaking circles,
6. victim panels that address offenders,
7. victim empathy classes for offenders, and
8. victim-directed and citizen-involved community service by the offender.

These programs provide higher levels of victim and offender satisfaction and a greater likelihood of successful restitution completion by the offender than traditional justice programs. "Research has also shown that restorative justice programs reduce fear among victims and decrease the frequency and severity of further criminal behavior among offenders" (Umbreit and Fercello 1997).

Restorative justice has been found to be very effective within the school systems because it offers a proactive alternative for administrators when addressing the involvement of youth in criminal activity. Rather than immediately expelling or suspending youth from school which in the past has been the norm and still common with many school administrators it gives them the option of offering a different way of making amends.

In the past when a student acted out they were often expelled from schools which drove them into the juvenile court system and juvenile corrections facilities never to return to school. For many their return meant to the streets and a life of petty crime. Restorative justice can be incorporated into school policies and practices and is very commonplace in many of the elementary, middle, and high schools throughout the country. Educators have become aware of the powerful impact and the success of this type of intervention. It has kept youths out of the juvenile justice system.

Restorative justice as a program creates opportunity for dialogue among all that are involved. The time to investigate the situation gives all the members involved the chance to review all of the possible reasons for the behavior or crimes and what may have been a factor in the incident. In the evaluation of the situation the school officials are given the opportunity to see whether the young adult had support needs that were not being met and the behavior was a direct result of these unmet needs. It is also very important to have the dialogue on how to make reparations while helping the young adult to find better alternatives and make better choices in the long run. "Schools can promote care and respect by providing restorative justice processes that allow for differences to be worked through in a constructive manner" (Morrison 2002).

WRAP-AROUND SERVICES

According to Leone, Quinn, and Osher (2002), "a preferred approach for reducing juvenile delinquency and crime is providing wrap-around services and supports through community-based, family-focused, and prevention-oriented collaboration, rather than incarcerating youth for longer periods of time," Wrap-around services are often nonexistent in many communities and are ill defined. These services need to be extremely well coordinated and accessible to be effective.

"Youth with disabilities as well as other youth within the juvenile justice system often need a wide range of individualized support. These services need to be comprehensive, collaborative, and available within the diverse communities and environments where these young adults live" (Stenhjem 2005). She goes on to emphasize the need for change in how services are delivered to a very fragile population.

It is a very sad reality that so many youths with special needs find themselves on the wrong side of the justice system. For many their disabilities are not taken into account when sentencing occurs. The law is very black and white. You do the crime you do the time. Detention centers are the last place that youths with special needs should be. They do not receive the necessary supports and intervention. Many of these youths do not have a rehabilitative experience. In fact, many are tragic statistics.

According to the Office of Juvenile Justice and Delinquency Prevention, in a report that was created in 1998, it was stated that "the most promising methods to prevent and reduce delinquency include addressing both risk factors (elements that increase the likelihood of delinquency) and protective factors (elements that insulate children considered at risk for juvenile delinquency) across numerous areas." Almost thirteen years later we are still striving to make progress on these recommendations.

Leone, Quinn, and Osher (2002) cite "the need for effective collaboration among key community agencies as a fundamental support for youth at risk for or engaged in violent juvenile behaviors." Almost every report that was investigated for this book indicated that collaboration among all interested parties was the key to success in any type of planning, service delivery or intervention.

Their model is based upon public health prevention, focusing on early identification, early intervention after onset, individualized services, and aftercare within collaborative systems of prevention, treatment, and care. It is a model that has been around for ten years, yet is still not fully implemented in many communities in America.

ALTERNATIVE HIGH SCHOOLS

The National Crime Prevention Council has put forth the idea that alternative high schools, often called learning academies, can be places of success for troubled youth. These schools are often small-scale school environments where a very limited number of students, sometimes less than twenty-five, receive intensive tutoring, consistent discipline with sanctions, counseling to establish goals for academic success and a transition to work, and guidance on developing life skills to cope with any special needs. These schools are meant to provide services and teaching in an alternative way that meets the needs of the student more concisely than a regular public school might.

The programs, run as separate entities of existing local high schools or as off-site programs (often referred to as the MALL Program), will serve students from several areas in the community or a juvenile court jurisdiction. The alternative schools usually require parents to give permission and at times sign off for their son or daughter to be placed in the environment. It is often presented to the parents as a last hope for their child to get a high school education. The programs can be voluntary or mandatory. If the program is mandatory there is a strong correlation that the youth has been involved with the juvenile justice system in some way (National Crime Prevention Council).

SCHOOL RESOURCE OFFICERS

Security officers, but most often state or local police officers, who have specialized training in youth or gang activities are a necessary presence on high school campuses throughout America. School counselors may also be trained in security as they are assigned to patrol school buildings during school hours. Their mandate is to develop positive relationships with students and staff, to recognize and respond to security threats on campus, and to deter crime through their visible presence in the school and at school-sponsored activities. They are seen as resources to all within the building. They are often the first line of defense in many conflict situations and can react and diffuse situations readily.

The officers may also sponsor or lead specific educational (drug prevention, conflict management) or recreational activities on campus as a means of building positive relationships with students. Some schools have established mentoring programs, pairing school resource officers with students who have discipline problems (National Crime Prevention Council).

BEFORE AND AFTER SCHOOL PROGRAMS

Many schools permit children to arrive early, when parents must leave for work, because otherwise the child would be unsupervised and/or alone within the home or the community. Schools have taken advantage of parents working to have children stay late in the afternoon to take advantage of tutoring, athletics, supervised programs, or playtime that builds on academic and social skills for children who may be lacking them.

Before- and after-school programs are usually run by college-age volunteers, school staff which may include the child's classroom teacher, or organizations willing to conduct programs at schools. They can also be based at community centers or church buildings with the support of the school community and district resources.

It is important that the program not be viewed as a baby-sitting service or an extension of school time, but rather a time during which children's developmental needs are served. Successful programs provide opportunities for play, creativity, companionship, and relaxation (National Crime Prevention Council).

TRAINING SCHOOL PERSONNEL IN CRIME PREVENTION

The National Crime Prevention Council has developed a very clear and concise program on how to train teachers. This violence prevention training builds the abilities of school personnel to prevent and respond to incidents in the school. Teachers should be trained in the following skills:

- improving the school climate through after-school activities
- conflict mediation
- recognizing the impact of social influences such as poverty and racism on student behavior
- promoting empathy among students for the concerns of others
- helping students control impulses to react violently when challenged teaching students problem-solving skills
- communicating with parents to get them to reinforce lessons from the classroom
- building self-esteem in students through praise and recognition
- using and teaching students to use resources in the community to address their needs.

Successful training programs for school staff also include training in implementing and enforcing school disciplinary and security procedures. Uniform application of these rules establishes a standard of behavior in the school and helps protect students, teachers, and staff (National Crime Prevention Council).

The key to success to any violence prevention program is in how well the staff that is trained adheres to the guidelines and implements them with fidelity. It is about being accountable and maintaining that high standard that will lead to safe environments for all.

GUN-FREE SCHOOL ZONES

Establishing policies prohibiting the possession of guns in schools and in communities goes a long way in preventing many gun related crimes. Community laws designate school buildings, school bus stops, and the perimeter area around school buildings as weapon-free zones, where possession or use of a firearm, knife, or other weapon carries additional penalties for the offender. In many states it is illegal to possess a weapon if you are a minor.

This strategy aims to deter offenders from carrying and using a gun or knife in the zone by imposing increased penalties. The penalties do not always discourage the youth offender but it may make them think twice about bringing a weapon to school. School and law enforcement officials believe that the policies are very effective in securing areas frequented by school-aged youth and staff while school is in session. It is unfortunate if a youth wants to bring a weapon to school he can find ways of concealing the weapon and enter the building. By having gun-free zones the discussion has begun and the expectations are put into place to have a safe school.

In addition to enhanced sanctions, most school districts where such policies are in place also have implemented antiviolence and gun education programs to reinforce among students the belief that carrying guns and knives to school is not safe and should not be tolerated by them and their peers. They have used education and awareness to change attitudes and behaviors (National Crime Prevention Council).

DIVERSITY AND TOLERANCE EDUCATION IN SCHOOLS

Teaching tolerance in elementary schools reduces the incidence of hate crimes, racism, discrimination, and bigotry. Children are aware of racial and gender differences at a very young age, and by age twelve they have formed stereotypes. In fact, recent studies show that tolerance education is most effective between the ages of four and nine years. Therefore, it is important to teach tolerance to young children and continue reinforcing the message over time.

Age-appropriateness is involved in the creation of the different curricula that educators have developed. For instance, part of the curriculum includes classroom exercises from newsletters and newspaper sections directed toward younger audiences. Additional methods include short theatrical productions and role-playing exercises (National Crime Prevention Council).

PROGRAM TYPES

The following programs have been researched and documented by the Office of Juvenile Justice and Delinquency Prevention (OJJDP). Each one of these alternative strategies has been well documented and has proven success with a variety of youth at risk. These strategies have been summarized here for the reader. Extended explanations can be found on the OJJDP website for the interested reader. The following summaries may be found at www.ojjdp.gov/mpg/programTypesDefinitions.aspx.

This text has been reproduced with the permission of the OJJDP.

1. Academic Skills Enhancement programs use instructional methods designed to increase student engagement in the learning process and hence increase their academic performance and bonding to the school (e.g., cooperative learning techniques and "experiential learning" strategies).
2. Aftercare is a re-integrative service that prepares out-of-home placed juveniles for reentry into the community by establishing the necessary collaborative arrangements with the community to ensure the delivery of prescribed services and supervision. A comprehensive aftercare process typically begins after sentencing and continues through incarceration and an offender's release into the community.
3. Afterschool/Recreation programs offer rewarding, challenging, and age-appropriate activities in a safe, structured, and positive environment. They may reduce delinquency by way of a socializing effect through which youth learn positive virtues such as discipline or simply reduce the opportunity for youth to engage in delinquency.
4. Alcohol and Drug Therapy / Education seeks to reduce the use or abuse of illegal drugs or alcohol by educating youth about the effects of drugs/alcohol. Programs in this category may take many forms, including 12-step programs such as Alcoholics Anonymous or Narcotics Anonymous, school-based and community-based prevention programs targeting alcohol, tobacco, or other drug use, and national public awareness campaigns.

5. Alternative School is essentially specialized educational environments that place a great deal of emphasis on small classrooms, high teacher-to-student ratios, individualized instruction, noncompetitive performance assessments, and less structured classrooms. The purpose of these schools is to provide academic instruction to students expelled or suspended for disruptive behavior or weapons possession, or who are unable to succeed in the mainstream school environment.

6. Classroom Curricula are classroom-based instruction programs designed to teach students factual information; increase their awareness of social influences to engage in misbehavior; expand their repertoires for recognizing and appropriately responding to risky or potentially harmful situation (e.g., drug use, gang involvement, violence); increase their appreciation for diversity in society; improve their moral character; improve conflict resolution skills; and encourage accountability.

7. Cognitive Behavioral Treatment seeks to correct an individual's faulty perceptions of themselves and/or the world around them. This type of therapy provides skills individuals can use to monitor their thought patterns and correct their behavior as situations unfold around them. Treatment may also focus on relapse prevention by having juveniles evaluate situations that may lead to a relapse of delinquent behavior, and then plan for how to either avoid them or cope with them effectively.

8. Community and Problem-Oriented Policing involves policing strategies designed to prevent crime by reducing opportunities and increasing the risks for engaging in criminal behavior through mutually beneficial ties between police and community members.

9. Community Awareness / Mobilization includes a broad array of community strategies designed to increase the development of broad, community-based crime prevention partnerships; increase public awareness of and support for crime prevention; and increase the capacity of diverse communities to deal with crime and victimization.

10. Conflict Resolution / Interpersonal Skills building refers to a wide range of processes that encourage nonviolent dispute resolution. In general, these processes teach young people decision-making skills to better manage conflict in juvenile facilities, schools, and communities. Youth learn to identify their interests, express their views, and seek mutually acceptable solutions to disputes. Common forms of conflict resolution include: negotiation, mediation, arbitration, community conferencing, and peer mediation. Similarly, interpersonal skill building focuses on developing the social skills required for an individual to interact in a positive way with others. The basic skills model begins

with an individual's goals, progresses to how these goals should be translated into appropriate and effective social behaviors, and concludes with the impact of the behavior on the social environment.

11. Correctional Facilities are public or private residential facilities with construction fixtures or staffing models designed to physically restrict the movements and activities of juveniles or other individuals. They are used for the placement, after adjudication and disposition, of any juvenile who has been adjudicated as having committed an offense, or of any other individual convicted of a criminal offense.

12. Day Treatment facilities (or day reporting centers) are highly structured, community-based, postadjudication, nonresidential programs for serious juvenile offenders. The goals of day treatment are to provide intensive supervision to ensure community safety and a wide range of services to the offender to prevent future delinquent behaviors. The intensive supervision is fulfilled by requiring the offender to report to the facility on a daily basis at specified times for a specified length of time. Generally, programs are provided at the facility during the day and/or evening at least 5 days a week. Special weekend activities may also be conducted.

13. Drug Court is a type of specialty court established within and supervised by juvenile courts to provide specialized services for eligible drug-involved youth and their families. In general, drug courts provide (1) intensive supervision over delinquency and status offense cases that involve substance-abusing juveniles and (2) coordinated and supervised delivery of an array of support services necessary to address the problems that contribute to juvenile involvement in the justice system. The services typically include: substance abuse treatment, mental health, primary care, family, and education.

14. Family Therapy focuses on improving maladaptive patterns of family interaction and communication. It is typically implemented with youth diagnosed with mild emotional and behavioral problems such as conduct disorder, depression, and school or social problems. The program is usually conducted by trained therapists in clinical settings with the parents and child.

15. Gang Prevention programs can be grouped into one of two categories. The first is gang membership prevention programs that try to prevent youth from joining gangs. The second is gang intervention programs that intercede with existing gang members during crisis conflict situations.

16. Group Homes are residential placements for juveniles that operate in a homelike setting in which a number of unrelated children live for varying time periods. Group homes may have one set of house parents

or may have a rotating staff. Some therapeutic or treatment group homes have specially-trained staff to assist children with emotional and behavioral difficulties.

17. Gun Court: A gun court is a type of specialty court that intervenes with youth who have committed gun offenses that have not resulted in serious physical injury. Most juvenile gun courts are short-term programs that augment rather than replace normal juvenile court proceedings.

18. Home Confinement w/without EM or house arrest with and without electronic monitoring (EM) is a community corrections program designed to restrict the activities of offenders in the community. This sanction allows offenders to remain in their homes, go to work, run errands, attend school, and maintain other responsibilities. However, their activities are closely monitored (either electronically and/or by frequent staff contacts) to ensure that they comply with the conditions set by the court. Offenders placed under home confinement are restricted to their residence for varying lengths of time and are required to maintain a strict schedule of daily activities.

19. Leadership and Youth Development programs prevent problem behaviors by preparing young people to meet the challenges of adolescence through a series of structured, progressive activities and experiences that help them obtain social, emotional, ethical, physical, and cognitive competencies. This approach views youth as resources and builds on their strengths and capabilities to develop within their own community. It focuses on the acquisition of adequate attitudes, behaviors, and skills.

20. Mentoring involves a relationship over a prolonged period of time between two or more people where an older, caring, more experienced individual provides help to the younger person as he or she goes through life. The goal of mentoring is to support the development of healthy individuals by addressing the need for positive adult contact and, thereby, reducing risk factors and enhancing protective factors for problem behavior.

21. Parent Training programs involve educating parents on specific management skills. This highly structured approach generally includes parents only, in small groups led by a skilled trainer or clinician. The program typically follows a curriculum guide and often includes video presentations of effective and ineffective ways of parenting; short lectures and discussions to identify parenting principles; interactive exercises; role-plays of direct practice in the parenting behavior to be changed; charting and monitoring of parenting and children's behavior and assignment of homework.

22. Probation Services refer to a variety of probation oriented programs, including traditional probation, intensive supervision and school-based probation. Traditional probation is a disposition in which youth are placed on informal/voluntary or formal/court ordered supervision. Intensive supervision programs (ISPs) are community-based, post adjudication, nonresidential programs designed to provide restraints on offenders in the community. School-based probation is a program partnership between juvenile probation departments and local schools that places probation officers directly within the confines of the school.

23. Reentry Court is a specialized court that manages the return of the offender to the community after being released from a residential placement. The court manages reentry by using its authority to apply graduated sanctions and positive reinforcement as well as direct resources to support the offender's reintegration and promote positive behavior.

24. Residential Treatment Centers (RTCs) are residential treatment facilities offering a combination of substance abuse and mental health treatment programs and 24-hour supervision in a highly structured (often staff-secure) environment. They usually house youth with significant psychiatric or substance abuse problems who have proved too ill or unruly to be housed in foster care, day treatment programs, and other nonsecure environments, but who do not yet merit commitment to a psychiatric hospital or secure corrections facility.

25. Although such treatment centers must be licensed by the state, they are frequently run by private, for-profit, and nonprofit institutions, and the treatment approaches and admissions criteria used by RTCs vary widely from state to state and institution to institution.

26. Restorative Justice is a theory of justice that emphasizes repairing the harm caused or revealed by criminal behavior. Practices and programs reflecting restorative purposes will respond to crime by (1) identifying and taking steps to repair harm, (2) involving all stakeholders, and (3) transforming the traditional relationship between communities and government in responding to crime. Some of the programs typically associated with restorative justice include: victim offender mediation, conferencing, circles, victim assistance, ex-offender assistance, restitution, and community service.

27. School/Classroom Environment programs seek to reduce or eliminate problem behaviors by changing the overall context in which they occur. These strategies may include interventions to change the decision-making processes or authority structures (building school capacity); redefining norms for behavior and signaling appropriate behavior

through the use of rules (setting norms for behavior); reorganizing classes or grades to create smaller units, continuing interaction, or different mixes of students, or to provide greater flexibility in instruction (classroom organization); and the use of rewards and punishments and the reduction of down time (classroom management).

28. Teen/Youth Court (or peer courts) are much like traditional courts in that there are prosecutors and defense attorneys, offenders and victims, and judges and juries, but young people rather than adults fill these roles and, most important, determine the disposition. The principal goal of a teen court is to hold young offenders accountable for their behavior by imposing sanctions that will repair some of the harm imposed on the victim and community.

29. Truancy Prevention is designed to promote regular school attendance through one or more strategies including an increase in parental involvement, the participation of law enforcement, the use of mentors, court alternatives, or other related strategies.

30. Vocational/Job Training programs address youth crime and unemployment by providing participants with social, personal, and vocational skills and employment opportunities to help them achieve economic success, avoid involvement in criminal activity, and subsequently increase social and educational functioning.

31. Wilderness Camps or challenge programs are generally residential placements that provide participants with a series of physically challenging activities, such as backpacking or rock climbing in an outdoor setting. These programs vary widely in terms of settings, types of activities, and therapeutic goals; but their treatment components are grounded in experiential learning which advocates "learning by doing" and facilitate opportunities for personal growth.

32. Wraparound / Case Management is a system of care that "wraps" a comprehensive array of individualized services and support around youth and their families to keep delinquent youth at home and out of institutions whenever possible. Treatment services are usually provided by multiple agencies working together as part of a collaborative interagency agreement, and each youth's treatment plan is determined by an interdisciplinary team consisting of a caseworker, family and community members, and several social services and mental health professionals. Individual case management is a less intense form of the wraparound approach where individual caseworkers guide youth through the existing social services or juvenile justice system and ensure that they receive appropriate services (OJJSP 2010).

Programs for juveniles delinquents have been numerous and available. What about very young offenders? There are children under twelve who are too young to be involved in incarceration or may not have the cognitive ability to truly understand their actions. Recent instances of children committing homicides have come to national attention and have attracted intense media scrutiny.

Despite the nationwide outrage in response to some of these cases, the number of juveniles age twelve or younger who are involved in murder is relatively small. Between 1980 and 1997, about 2 percent (or six hundred cases) of murders involved such child offenders, and the annual number of these murders was relatively stable, averaging about thirty per year.

According to the FBI's Supplementary Homicide Reports (Snyder 2001), the large majority (84 percent) of children who were aggressors and murdered other individual are males. Seventy percent of the murder victims of child delinquents were male and likely to be acquaintances or family members. More than one-half (54 percent) of the murder victims of child delinquents were killed with a firearm. These statistics are both horrendous and totally unnecessary. We need to educate and prevent access to firearms.

"The most promising school and community prevention programs for child delinquency focus on several risk domains" (Herrenkohl et al. 2001). It is important to fully understand the problem before one can address it effectively. These risks domains are great predictors for future violence and acting out on the part of troubled youth.

Several government agencies who are on the front line in dealing with child delinquency recommend integrating the following types of school and community prevention programs.

These additional program recommendations were also highlighted in the Office of Juvenile Justice and Delinquency Programs Report. This text has been reproduced with permission of the OJJDP.

1. Classroom and behavior management programs. Children spend a lot of time in the classroom; by structuring the lessons and discussions in a safe environment, the children should learn appropriate behaviors in the correct context.
2. Multicomponent classroom-based programs are instrumental in teaching children how to understand their emotions and their behaviors. Within the school environment there are many different areas that can be used to teach the child new skills. The opportunity to generalize their learning is frequent and well monitored.
3. Social competence promotion curriculums empower students to learn new social skills that they can generalize to their everyday life in and

out of school. These curriculums can enable the child to role play in a safe environment and learn which skills are the social norms in that community.

4. Conflict resolution and violence prevention curriculums enable children to understand how to regulate and understand their emotions. They become better able to mediate their problems and learn a system of conflict resolution other than one based in violence.

5. Bullying prevention programs are nationwide and abundant. There are several programs that recently have focused on teaching and educating both teachers and students on how to prevent bullying, how to report bullying and how not to be a victim of bullying.

6. Afterschool recreation programs have been instrumental in guiding children to leave the street and stay in a protected environment where they are supervised and guided to learn and participate in safe activities. These recreational activities have been known to teach as well as counsel children who are having difficulties.

7. Mentoring programs have given specific vocational and interest based skills to children who may not have had any type of goal or direction in their life. These programs have exposed and introduced troubled children with hope and promise at having a possible career or just positive adult or youth role models.

8. School organization programs have helped children to have choices to funnel their energy beyond criminal activity. These programs have allowed children to become involved in positive ways and to be connected to their school. It has allowed children to build a sense of school pride and to belong to something that values their participation.

9. Comprehensive community interventions have become important in reclaiming a community from drug and crime infested behaviors. The rebirth of some communities by regaining control and driving out the negative factors that could and do influence children to a life of crime have been eradicated and replaced with positive actions and programs that have offered children new options and new hope. Several of these unique programs have demonstrated that interventions with young children can reduce later delinquency.

10. Common Sense Parenting (CSP) is a group-based parent training class designed for parents of youth ages 6–16 who exhibit significant behavior and emotional problems. The objective of the program is to teach positive parenting techniques and behavior management strategies to help increase positive behavior, decrease negative behavior, and model appropriate alternative behavior for children. The program consists of six weekly 2-hour sessions involving a group

of 10–12 parents led by certified trainers who work from a detailed trainer's manual. The session topics are: Parents Are Teachers, Encouraging Good Behavior, Preventing Problems, Correcting Problem Behavior, Teaching Self-Control, and Putting It All Together. Common Sense Parenting classes concentrate on experiential learning and consist of five training components—review, instruction, modeling, practice, and feedback—and conclude with a summary. Each session is designed to teach one parenting concept and a skill related to that concept.

During each training session, parents review the skills learned during the previous session, receive instruction in a new parenting skill, view videotaped models of the new skill, practice how to use the skill in simulated role-play, and receive feedback from the trainer. Parenting skills and techniques are taught to be adapted by parents for use in any home environment. Parents learn skills such as the use of clear communication, positive reinforcements and consequences, self-control, and problem-solving (OJJDP 2010).

There are additional programs that have also had documented success in dealing with youths that are violent or are involved in criminal activities. This author is not endorsing any of these programs but is providing their program components for reference or information purposes only.

CeaseFire Chicago is a Chicago, Illinois–based violence-prevention program administered by the Chicago Project for Violence Prevention since the program began in 1999. CeaseFire uses an evidence-based public health approach to reduce shootings and killings by using highly trained street violence interrupters and outreach workers, public education campaigns, and community mobilization. Rather than aiming to directly change the behaviors of a large number of individuals CeaseFire concentrates on changing the behavior and risky activities of a small number of selected members of the community who have a high chance of either "being shot" or "being a shooter" in the immediate future.

The activities of CeaseFire are organized into five core components, which address both the community and those individuals who are most at risk of involvement in a shooting or killing:

1. Street-level outreach going out in the streets to reach the clients.
2. Public education in multiple forms to build knowledge and skills.
3. Community mobilization to get everyone in the community to care and become involved.
4. Faith leader (clergy) involvement gives a sense of faith and moral guidance.

5. Police and prosecutor participation get everyone involved in the juvenile system to become stakeholders (OJJDP 2010).

CeaseFire's interventions are based on a theory of behavior that specifies the information data that needs to be assembled and set in motion and how they cause the "outcomes," including reductions in shootings and killings. Many of the program's daily activities target the causal factors linking inputs to outcomes, which were presumed to be among the major determinates of violence. The research this program has done has discovered that there are several causal factors that are believed to contribute to violence. They may include but are not limited to the community norms that are the standard expectation, availability of on-the-spot alternatives for youth to be involved in or have access to instead of resorting to violence when the situation arises, and the youth's awareness of the risks and costs associated with violence.

First, the program aims at changing the local norms regarding violence. They begin by working in both the wider community and among its clients through a variety of ways. This may include trying a community mobilization where community members are made aware of the issues and concerns. It may be a well-defined public education campaign that targets core parts of the community. It may be through mentoring efforts of outreach workers who are calculated to influence beliefs about the appropriateness of violence. It may begin with conversations one on one. Outreach workers are charged with stimulating a level of change among clients and guiding them toward alternatives rather than using violence or shootings as a way of solving problems. It provides the youth with some level of choice and education about making informed and appropriate decisions.

Outreach workers counsel a small group of young clients, who are recruited from the streets and not through institutions, and connect them to a range of services. The reasons being this is to have youths talk to other youths. It has been proved that kids listen to other kids if they believe the youth has credibility through their experiences.

Workers also conduct a significantly high number of conflict mediations as a way to model problem solving strategies and positive resolution to conflict that does not involve violence. The efforts of the clergy and residents of the community are also aimed primarily at norm change, both in the community and among clients of the outreach workers and other high-risk youth.

Community involvement also targets the perceived costs of violence. People become informed through very specific data and evidence. The public education campaign is aimed at both changing norms about violence and enhancing the perceived risks of engaging in violence. It gives a realistic perspective of the overall costs of violence in a community.

Second, the program provides on-the-spot alternatives to violence when gangs and individuals on the street are making behavior decisions. This program is in the streets and present. They are there to act when needed. The program treats young people as rational actors capable of making choices, and the strategy is to promote their consideration of a broader array of response to situations that too often elicit shootings and killings as a problem-solving tactic. The expression of respect and problem solving mediation techniques are shown to be effective and can be better choices than extreme violence.

Violence interrupters work on the streets alone or in pairs to mediate conflicts between gangs and stem the cycle of retaliatory violence that threatens to break out following a shooting. It provides an alternative to just going out and killing for revenge.

Violence interrupters work the street in the night talking to gang leaders, distraught friends and relatives of recent shooting victims, and others who are positioned to initiate or sustain cycles of violence. Their presence is a positive resource available to youths to explore their options and make a better choice.

Finally, the program aims to increase the perceived risks and costs of involvement in violence among high-risk, largely young people. This reflects a classic deterrence model of human behavior, with risks such as incarceration, injury, and death highlighted for youth. Actions by the police and prosecutors, as well as tougher antigun legislation, are seen as targeting the risks surrounding involvement in shootings (OJJDP 2010).

Family Centered Treatment (FCT) is a treatment model designed for use in the provision of intensive in-home services. FCT is especially well suited for high-risk juveniles who are not responding to typical community-based services or who have been found to need institutional placement, as well as those returning from incarceration or institutional placement.

A primary goal of FCT is to keep the youth in the community and divert them from further penetration into the juvenile justice system. FCT is different from other traditional in-home family therapy or counseling programs in that it is family focused rather than client focused. Treatment services concentrate on providing a foundation that maintains family integrity, capitalizes on the youth's and family's inherent resources (i.e., skills, values, and communication patterns), develops resiliency, and demands responsibility and accountability.

FCT was first developed because practitioners wanted to have at their disposal simple, practical, and commonsense solutions for families faced with forced removal of their children from the home or dissolution of the family. Often times the removal was due to external and internal stressors and circumstances that were unclear or confusing to the parents.

The basic framework for treatment draws from components of evidence-based models such as Eco Structural Family Therapy developed by Aponte in 1976 and Emotionally Focused Therapy developed by Johnson and Greenberg in 1985. These individuals were the front runners and pioneers in trying to solve the problem.

FCT is a model of treatment that integrates behavioral change with a primary emphasis on value change for the members of the system. A fundamental premise of FCT is that youth and their families' long-term changes are predicated upon their valuing the changes made, because changes made for compliance or conformity are not sustainable after treatment ends.

Program services include case management, supervision, group meetings, outreach services, crisis prevention/intervention services, and community services. Treatment is conducted in natural settings (i.e., in the home, school, or community), and typically lasts about six months, with several hours of contact in multiple sessions every week. FCT is structured into four phases:

1. Joining and Assessment. The Family Centered Specialist (FCS) engages and gains acceptance by the family and works with them to identify areas that affect their functioning.
2. Restructuring. The FCS and family use experiential practice to alter ineffective behavioral patterns among family members. This process includes techniques to modify the crisis cycle to more adaptive patterns of family functioning.
3. Value Change. Through powerful emotional intervention techniques, family members integrate new behaviors into their personal value systems to create long-term change. Giving to others or back to the community is integral in this phase.
4. Generalization. With new skills for dealing with conflict and increased understanding of its own dynamics, the family continues its work, but the treatment is less intense and frequent. The focus is on practice, review of what has worked previously, and reversals (OJJDP 2010).

The model allows the flexibility to move back and forth between the restructuring and value change phases in order to respond to individual family dynamics. The FCS transitions the family from one phase into the next phase as the family demonstrates behaviors reflective of the key indicators of change (OJJDP 2010).

Preparing for the Drug Free Years (PDFY) is a program for parents of children in grades four through eight that was developed by Hawkins and Catalano, whose main goal was to design a program that reduced adolescent drug use and behavior problems. PDFY's skill-based curriculum enables parents to identify and address risks that can and often will contribute to drug abuse while trying to strengthen family bonding by building protective factors like trust, awareness and relationship building.

PDFY is well embedded in the social development model which emphasizes that young people should experience opportunities for active involvement in the family where they are involved and connected to these individuals. Young people in schools should feel protected. When in their community they should be able to be functioning members, and develop skills for success, and should be given recognition and reinforcement for positive effort and improvement.

PDFY focuses on strengthening family bonds and establishing clear standards for behavior that are clearly articulated and defined. This creates a plan to help parents manage their child's behavior while encouraging their development. The ultimate goal of PDFY is to reach parents before their children begin experimenting with drugs. The core curriculum of the family sessions is to focus and build family relationships and communication where specific skills are taught, reinforced and practice with a certain amount of success.

The curriculum also helps parents to build their family management skills such as giving directions and commands, requests and follow through when dealing with difficult situations. Since many parents do not have a skill set around resolution of family conflict they are coached on how to deal effectively with conflict that leads to successful resolution rather than additional conflict (Hawkins and Catalano 1999).

The Homebuilders Program is one of the best documented Intensive Family Preservation Programs in the country. The program is designed to break the cycle of family dysfunction by strengthening families, keeping children safe, and preventing foster care, residential and other forms of out-of-home placement. This program's main goal is to build family engagement, support and keep families together as much as possible. It is a lofty goal but is doable and realistic.

The program goals have clearly been articulated and developed. They may include some or all of the following as part of the individual and family program. Each individual family's plan may include improving family functioning; increasing social support; increasing parenting skills; preventing or reducing child abuse and neglect; improving school and job attendance and performance; improving household living conditions; establishing daily routines; improving adult and child self-esteem; helping clients become self-directed; and enhancing motivation for change while decreasing family conflict and other problems.

The program values the importance of meeting and taking parents and family units where they are at and building the necessary skills that will lead to a more successful family unit. The program is designed for the most seriously troubled families, especially those that have experienced assault, abuse and neglect and even victimization who are referred by a number of child service agencies. Populations served include newborns to teenagers, and their families. If the family is in crisis there is a very good possibility that they will qualify.

The program includes four to six weeks of intensive, in-home services to children and families. A practitioner with a caseload of two families provides counseling, hard services, develops community support, and spends an average of eight to ten hours per week in direct contact with the family, and is on call twenty-four hours a day, seven days a week for crisis intervention. There is always a back-up team to provide the necessary support and intervention when needed.

The program utilizes a single practitioner model with a team back-up for co-therapy and consultation. Teaching strategies involve modeling, descriptions of skills and behaviors, role plays and rehearsals of newly acquired skills. Teaching tools include skills-based video- and audio-tapes, work books, handouts, articles and exercises. "Therapeutic processes used are skill building, behavioral interventions, motivational interviewing, relapse prevention, rational emotive therapy, and other cognitive strategies" (Booth 2002).

In the last few years diversion programs have become very popular in many states as a way of dealing with juvenile offenders. Diversion is "an attempt to divert, or channel out, youthful offenders from the juvenile justice system" (Bynum and Thompson 1996: 430). "The concept of diversion is based on the theory that processing certain youth through the juvenile justice system may do more harm than good" (Lundman 1993).

The basis of the diversion argument is that courts may stigmatize some youth for having committed relatively petty acts that might best be handled outside the formal system. Not all youths need to come in front of a court of law. It is not the best use of court or justice time. In part, diversion programs are also designed to ameliorate the problem of overburdened juvenile courts and overcrowded corrections institutions (including detention facilities), so that courts and institutions can focus on more serious offenders.

GOALS AND OBJECTIVES OF DIVERSION PROGRAMS

The major goals of the program are to reduce the number of youth in court-ordered detention and provide youth with culturally relevant community-based services and supervision. Diversion program provides an intensive level of community-based monitoring and advocacy not available within the traditional juvenile justice system. Specific diversion program objectives include the following:

- Ensuring that a high proportion of program clients are not rearrested while participating in the program.
- Ensuring that youth appear in court as scheduled.
- Reducing the population of the Youth Guidance Center (the juvenile court), currently the only place of juvenile detention in the city.
- Providing interventions for youth diverted from secure detention facilities.
- Demonstrating that community-based interventions are an effective alternative to secure custody and can meet the needs of both the youth and the community at a cost savings to the public.
- Reducing disproportionate minority incarceration (including detention) (CJCJ 2010).

There is still some additional research that needs to be conducted on the effectiveness of diversion programs. The goals are the pathways to changing how we deal with youth offenders. There has to be a better way because what we have been doing for decades is not working.

Youth Advocate Programs, Inc. (YAP) provides a community-based alternative to placement for juvenile probation departments. The goals and mission of this program is strength-based, family-focused program that serve adjudicated juvenile offenders whose behavior and social circumstances put them at risk of placement in residential facilities. Many of these youths would not survive or would be attacked and assaulted within an institution or a juvenile detention center. Eligible youth are those deemed by the courts to be in need of residential care for multiple reasons that are assessed and part of the evaluation report. The program follows an innovative advocacy/wraparound model that includes a comprehensive mix of highly individualized services for youth and their families. The program goals are to:

- Decrease the occurrence of juvenile crime and enhance community safety;
- Increase opportunities for success and improve quality of life for youth and families; and
- Facilitate community empowerment (Youth Advocate Program).

YAP today provides programs for high-risk youth and their families in Texas, Florida, South Carolina, New York, New Jersey, Ohio, Pennsylvania, Arizona, Louisiana, and the District of Columbia (Youth Advocate Program).

THE S.T.A.R. PROGRAM

The program is used by schools and juvenile judges as an alternative to suspension, expulsion out of school detention and other more expensive and less effective disciplinary tools. Students placed in the Student Transition and Recovery Program are required to attend their normal classes at their normal schools and return home each evening. In the morning before school and in the afternoon after school, students participate in exercises, counseling, tutoring, and military-style drills. Throughout the school day S.T.A.R. Instructors check on the students in their classes and during lunch to ensure appropriate behavior. The youths in this program are monitored frequently and made accountable for their behavior no matter where they are. There is no escaping or avoiding accepting responsibility.

This program has been grouped in the boot camp list of alternatives. This type of program has had several controversies attached to it and has been found to be abusive in some areas of the United States. However, some of these programs have had remarkable successes with at-risk youth. It was included in this section for information purposes only.

The Mountain Homes Youth Ranch Program is divided into three phases and is defined by specific benchmarks that need to be accomplished at each stage. In the beginning phase, participants learn the interdependency of nature's resources, personal skill and knowledge, and responsible and cooperative behavior for the sustaining of life's basic needs. They become attuned to what nature can offer as part of a recovery program. They become more aware of themselves and their environment. As participants learn ancient Indian skills using the resources of nature, they begin to develop an awareness of themselves regarding their abilities and the values of cooperation and responsibility to the community in meeting basic life needs. They become one with nature.

The advanced phase of the program continues to place youth in a camping community where everyone shares responsibility for community living equally. Emphasis is placed on the interdependency of community members through using skills learned in the beginning phase in a cooperative effort to sustain peaceful and productive life in a family setting. They begin to understand that they are not alone, that they do not need to fight others to become part of a group or to find peace and fulfillment of basic needs.

Participants continue individual and group counseling as new perspectives on old values and assumptions begin to become internalized. The therapeutic relationship and healing is ongoing and develops at a rate that is comfortable for the individual to begin changing some of their attitudes or to make a total shift in their paradigm.

The ranch phase of the program emphasizes working with the family group as a unit. The student learns the value of trust and integrity, and that within the unit each person's actions affect everyone. They begin understanding that we are all interdependent.

The skills learned in the first two phases help teach the student independence and leadership, which they utilize in their scholastic venues such as

GED, high school and college correspondence courses. They begin seeing the value of what higher education can bring in terms of success and reintegration into society.

Within this phase participants continue to communicate directly with their parents in a conference call designed to work on communication and integration back into their home environment. During the final two days of ranch, parents are given the opportunity to attend the graduation and a parenting seminar and are invited to tour the on-site facilities (Mountain Homes Ranch Webpage).

The focus of this chapter was to provide a variety of resources and programs that individuals working and interacting with juvenile and child delinquents could use to investigate options for interventions. In no way does this author endorse one program over another. Each program has some uniqueness that may make it successful with one child and unsuccessful with another. There are many factors that need to be evaluated and documented before one program is chosen over another. Some of these programs are for individual children and youths, others for schools and school districts, and others for communities. The important thing to remember is that there are options and all individuals involved with this population of troubled youth can take action and be preventative in making sure that another youth or child at risk does not become a statistic or a fatality our of society.

10

International Perspectives

How America Compares to the World

We often hear and see in the media how America is a cesspool of violence and crime. That Americans overall are extremely narcissistic and prone to violence at a drop of a dime. The United States of America is known as a violent society because there are few sanctions to prevent the outbursts of violence by children and youths.

In fact this culture encourages violence by giving children and youths rights of expression and free speech. One of the issues is that youth are taught early on that they need to protect themselves in whichever way they can because the mentality is "kill or be killed."

The reality is that very few American youth think this way. If they are part of a gang culture or live in a very violent community this is the norm. However, the vast majority of American youth are law abiding citizens who do the right thing. They are models of good citizenship and character. It is but a small part of the population that resorts to violence to solve their problem or to achieve power.

One of the issues around child and youth violence internationally is that there are various ages of criminal responsibility which therefore leads to a variety of responses. In some countries there are different ages for boys and girls. Below is just a sampling of these ages of criminal responsibility. Some countries put children as young as seven into the criminal justice system; others don't assign criminal responsibility until age sixteen. These are the minimum ages at which children are subject to penal law in various countries:

- 7—India, South Africa, Thailand, Pakistan, Myanmar, Sudan
- 8—Scotland, Kenya, Indonesia

- 9—Ethiopia, Iran (girls only)
- 10—England, Wales, Ukraine, Nepal
- 11—Turkey
- 12—South Korea, Morocco, Uganda, Canada
- 13—France, Algeria, Poland
- 14—Germany, China, Italy, Japan, Russia, Vietnam
- 15—Egypt
- 16—Argentina

Due to this discrepancy worldwide we are seeing a variety of interventions in a variety of countries that do not always seem just in the eyes of other nations.

The focus of this chapter is to highlight that crime and violence does occur in other countries. The difference is that the media does not sensationalize it to the same degree as they do in America. Below you will read a series of international crimes that speak to the fact that violence is alive and well everywhere in the world. These cases are all from the headlines of major newspapers in the respective countries. They are actual newspaper accounts as reported by the writers for the population of that country and the world to read. These stories are summarized and do not reflect the whole article. I have included the links so that if you would like to read the full articles you are welcome to investigate the full story.

UNITED KINGDOM

In the United Kingdom almost 3,000 crimes were reported last year where the suspect was too young to be prosecuted, the British Broadcasting Corporation has learned. Figures show about 1,300 incidents of criminal damage and arson, and more than 60 sex offences where suspects were under-10s in England and Wales. If a child is nine or under in the United Kingdom, he or she cannot be charged with an offence but there are calls for the age of criminal responsibility to be lowered. The figures are based on data from 32 of the 43 forces in England and Wales. Of the 2,840 crimes where the suspect was under 10, about half were cases of arson or criminal damage.

There were also 66 sexual offences, including a number of sexual assaults on children under 13. The figures, obtained by BBC Radio Five Live through requests under the Freedom of Information Act, also show children too young to face charges were suspected of harassment, wounding and burglary. As a proportion of total crime the numbers are small. Home Office figures show there were 5.5 million incidents reported to the police during the same period (http//news.bbc.co.uk/2/hi/6974587.stm (2007)).

One of the biggest news stories also came out of the UK.

In February 1993 two year old James Bulger was abducted and murdered by two ten year old boys, Robert Thompson and Jon Venables. James went missing while out shopping with his mother in Bootle's Strand Shopping Centre on 12 February 1993.

Thompson and Venables led James away from the shopping centre while his mother was in a nearby butcher's shop. The picture, captured on CCTV, of James Bulger being led away by hand was to become one of the most infamous images of the case.

After murdering James the boys left his body on a nearby railway line where it was discovered two days later. The investigation was led by Detective Superintendent Albert Kirby. After their arrest and throughout the trial the boys were known only as Child A and Child B.

In November 1993 Thompson and Venables were convicted of the murder of James Bulger. The boys were named by the trial judge Mr. Justice Morland and sentenced to secure youth accommodation with a recommendation that they serve at least eight years in jail. In June 2001 Thompson and Venables were released on life license and given new, secret identities.

The details of the murder that emerged during the trial shocked many people and led to public outrage, particularly in Bootle and Liverpool.

After abducting James the boys had walked him for two and a half miles. They were seen by 38 people, some of whom challenged them, the boys claiming that they were looking after their younger brother or that James was lost and they were taking him to a local police station.

Since their release an injunction in England and Wales has banned reporting of Thompson and Venable's new names and their whereabouts. Although the ban does not apply in Scotland, or other countries, and despite numerous rumors their identities have remained secret.

Here is a detailed account of what supposedly happened that day when James was abducted: Jon and Robert left the Liverpool shopping center and walked up Stanley Road. They carried the toddler, who was crying. They set him down near the post office and said loudly, "Are you all right? You were told not to run." James cried for his mother, but the boys continued on, ignoring him. Jon held the boy's hand as they walked. Sometimes he ran ahead; other times he fell behind. They walked down to the canal and under a bridge to an isolated area.

Jon and Robert joked about pushing James into the water. It was at the canal that they first hurt James. One of them (each blamed the other) picked James up and dropped him on his head. They had their opportunity and had made their first assault on the toddler. Yet Jon and Robert ran away, afraid. They weren't prepared to kill, so they left James alone by the canal, crying loudly.

A woman saw James and assumed he was with some other children nearby. Jon and Robert turned around and walked back toward James. "Come on, baby." In his utter innocence, little James with a big bruise and cut on his forehead, once again followed his tormentors. They covered the child's head with the hood of his anorak so that his wound would be less visible.

Holding James's hand, they walked back toward Stanley Road and crossed at a busy intersection. After returning from the canal, the boys seemed to have lost their purpose and their direction. They meandered, strolling past shops, halls, offices, and car parks. A witness on a bus saw the two boys, swinging the toddler's hands, as he walked between them. A motorist later saw the boys pulling the baby, against his will. He was crying and did not want to go further. He saw Robert kick the baby in the ribs. "A persuading kick," the witness later described it. Jon, Robert, and James had walked over a mile by now, along a busy road in Liverpool.

It was late afternoon. At another crossing James began to cry for his mother again. He ran off and almost ran into traffic, but Robert caught him and pulled him back. Motorists watched the boys as they crossed the street and could see that James was crying, dragging his heels. Some thought James was crying because he was not allowed to run free.

Jon carried James by the legs, while Robert held him by the chest. They awkwardly carried the boy to a grassy plateau by a reservoir where they sat on a step and rested, placing James between them. A woman walking her dog passed them by and noticed that little James was laughing. But moments later, another person saw Jon punch James, grabbing him and violently shaking him.

For some inexplicable reason, this witness pulled her curtains, shutting out the scene. It was growing dark. At the grassy knoll by the reservoir, an elderly woman noticed the baby, who was obviously hurt. She approached them and asked what the problem was. James was in tears, his face bruised and red. "We just found him at the bottom of the hill," Jon and Robert claimed as if they didn't know him. She told the boys to take him to the Walton Lane Police Station just down the road and gave them directions there.

The little boy's injuries worried her. She pointed them in the direction of the police, but watched incredulously as they walked off in the opposite direction. She shouted after them, but they didn't turn back. As she stood there, unsure what to do, another woman who had seen the boys earlier said that James had been laughing. She believed the baby was okay; they were probably inexperienced brothers watching over their younger sibling. Later that night, the woman saw the news of the missing toddler on television. She immediately called the police and told them about her encounter. "I wish now I had done something," she said (Coslett 2006).

MEXICO–USA BORDER

A 17-year-old Mexican was sentenced to 40 years in prison Thursday for murdering a U.S. Border Patrol agent who was lured from his vehicle during an attempted robbery and shot repeatedly in the head.

Defendant Christian Daniel Castro Alvarez, described as a one-time smuggler of illegal immigrants, sat with his head down throughout the hearing, as the wife and sisters of 30-year-old Robert Rosas emotionally described how his execution shattered their lives.

Castro wrote a letter, read in court by the judge, saying he was "extremely sorry" and wished he could turn back the clock. . . .

Rosas was shot eight times in the head, neck and torso while on solo patrol the night of July 23, 2009 in a rugged, remote mountainous area near Campo, about 60 miles east of San Diego. He was shot repeatedly from behind. . . .

Castro told authorities he and his collaborators lured Rosas out of his vehicle by leaving footprints on a dirt road, shaking bushes and making noise. Castro said he was holding Rosas at gunpoint when the agent reached for Castro's firearm.

Castro, then 16, said he shot once and shouted to his collaborators for help as they walked toward Rosas' vehicle. They turned and opened fire. (Spagat 2010)

This crime was brutal and for no apparent reason except that Rosas was doing his job.

GERMANY

BERLIN (UPI)—An increased perception of violence by immigrant youth has sparked a debate about ethnic youth crime in Germany that divides the government in Berlin.

Most Germans have seen this video, whether on YouTube or on national television: Two young men are punching and kicking the head of a pensioner who is lying motionless on the concrete floor of a Munich subway station. Then, one of the men steps back takes up speed and kicks the head once more in full running. The kid kicks so hard that he has to hold his foot in pain. (Nicola 2008)

A second report indicated that a pensioner was hit on the head and knocked out Wednesday in Germany in an attack involving minority youths, further heating up debate about violence by immigrants.

The man, who was accompanied by his wife, had told off three men who were vandalizing a memorial plaque to a policewoman shot dead last year in the line of duty in the south-western city of Heilbronn. He was hit by the men, fainted and was admitted to hospital.

Police in a helicopter and squad cars rounded up the accused, a 19-year-old Bosnian, a 16-year-old Turk and a 22-year-old German national. Police said the trio were drunk, had molested several other people and were repeat trouble-makers.

Germans are debating a crackdown after an incident last month in which two minority youths cracked the skull of a retired school principal for telling them to obey a Munich smoking ban.

In other cases, train passengers were punched for asking minority youths to turn down loud music. State leaders have called for "warning-shot" detention for hooligans and instant deportation if those convicted do not hold German nationality. (en.trend.az/news/world/news/1108436.html)

AUSTRALIA

Thugs recruited to settle a school playground dispute have ambushed students on their way home from classes in two separate attacks.

While a public high school was under police guard after a serious assault, five youths followed a bus and attacked a student as he got off at Kings Langley in Sydney's west.

The incident came three days after 20 attackers said to have been armed with planks containing exposed nails viciously bashed three Crestwood High School students at Baulkham Hills last Friday.

One victim, aged 17, suffered a fractured eye socket and broken nose.

Police later charged a male, 16, who is not a Crestwood student, with assaulting a student, assault occasioning actual bodily harm and affray. He was bailed to appear in Parramatta Children's Court on March 11.

In the Kings Langley assault, about 4pm on Monday, police said the attackers targeted the wrong student. "They accosted a young kid of 16 or 17 - he got a bit of a graze to his knee when they pushed to him to the ground," Detective Chief Inspector Wayne Murray said.

He said police believed the incident was linked to Friday's attack and are looking for a dark green hatchback. "It . . . stems from an escalation from some sort of altercation that occurred at school between a Year 11 student and a Year 12 student," he said. "There was a recruitment of kids from outside the area to settle a playground dispute."

Up to eight police cars as well as private security guards and teachers have been patrolling the perimeter of Crestwood High School.

On Tuesday a teacher disarmed a knife-wielding primary student as police were called to Claremont Meadows School in western Sydney.

But Education Minister Verity Firth yesterday denied there was any surge in violence at schools and ruled out metal detectors or security searches, claiming schools had adequate powers to deal with violent children including mandatory 20-day suspensions and anti-bullying programs. (*Daily Telegraph* 2010)

JAPAN

Over the past few years, the people of Japan have been shocked by a series of horrific crimes committed by teenagers. It started in 1997 in the city of Kobe, when a 14-year-old killed a younger boy and cut his head off. He left the head outside a school, along with a taunting note. He was eventually arrested, but not before killing another boy. Another teenager murdered an entire family of neighbors and a 17-year-old killed a woman with a knife, during a bus hijack.

Ruriko Take lost her 16-year-old son four years ago, when a group of teenagers beat and kicked him to death. She was horrified when a family court sent one of the killers to a Juvenile Training School for less than a year. She explains:

"If a young person takes someone's life, they usually don't face a criminal trial. They are not punished. But who takes responsibility for ending that life? … The Juvenile Law here only deals with the problems of offenders – how to protect them and rehabilitate them. The sufferings of the victims are not taken into account at all." (Levinson 2001)

During the spring and summer of 1997, Japan was rocked by a hideous crime. On May 27th, several people spotted what appeared to be a manikin's head resting in front of the gate to one of the local junior high schools in the port city of Kobe. Once someone examined the scene closer, they realized the head was not a fake at all. It belong to Jun Hase, an 11 year old mentally challenged boy who had been missing for several days. Inside the mouth, there was a note that read: "Well, let's begin a game. Can you stop me, police? I desperately want to see people die. I think it is fun to kill people. A bloody judgment is needed for my years of great bitterness."

A rash of crimes had hit that area lately. A 10 year old girl had been beaten to death with a steel pipe in March and a 9 year old girl was stabbed the same day. Before that, 2 other school girls were attacked by someone with a hammer. Along with human victims, 2 dead animals had been found near the school. One was a bird who was decapitated and the other a kitten who had its paws cut off.

Knowing they had a serial killer on their hands, the police started looking for the last person seen with young Jun. He had been a man in his 30s. In the month of June, the killer started sending letters to local newspapers. In these letters he claimed that murder brought him an inner peace. He went on to say he would kill 3 children a week.

Finally at the end of June the killer was caught. Instead of joy, there was shock. The killer turned out to be a 14 year old boy. Like many serial killers before him, he started showing signs at an early age. He enjoyed torturing animals, played around with hunting knives. Once he lined frogs up on the street and ran them over with his bike. He kept a detailed journal of his crimes and rituals. After luring Jun to a wooded hill, he strangled him and removed his head with a saw. Afterwards, he took the head home where he washed it in a purification ceremony before leaving it at the school gate.

Under Japanese law, the killer could not be jailed because of his age. One way or another he is expected to be back on the streets by the time he is 18. Based on that information, in 2001 he would have turned 18. (http://deadsilence. wordpress.com/2006/07/15/the-kobe-school-killer/)

TOKYO: Four-year-old Shun Tanemoto told his mother he would be in the video game department as they shopped in an electronics store last week. When she came to fetch him a few minutes later, he was gone. His body, stripped naked, was found the next morning, apparently thrown from a high parking garage.

The crime caused headlines, but when Nagasaki police traced images on a security camera, the result was even more disturbing. The photos showed another boy, wearing a school uniform, leading the young child away. On Wednesday, police announced that a 12-year-old schoolboy, described as "a good student," had confessed to the kidnapping and murder.

For Japan, the story came as yet another of the periodic reminders that the society is not as safe as its storied reputation suggests. And this incident, involving such young children, has prompted an unusual cry for vengeance. Shun's parents, distraught that the alleged killer is too young to be tried in criminal court in Japan, wished the death penalty could be used on the 12 year old.

A government minister, Yoshitada Konoike, said the alleged murderer's parents ought to suffer a medieval punishment. "The parents should be dragged through the streets and beheaded," Konoike said. "Then parents and their children would be more careful."

Such violent prescriptions are unusual in debate here, where murder is considered an aberration and society still sees itself as uniquely law-abiding and safe. There has been little public debate about Japan's steady 14-year climb in violent crime, now at its highest level since 1968, except to blame foreigners, who contribute a statistically minuscule part of the rise. In 1997 a 14-year-old boy in Kobe cut off the head of an 11-year-old and left it outside a school gate.

In 2000, a 15-year-old stabbed three neighbors to death in southwestern Japan. In 2001, an 11-year-old stabbed his mother to death. . . .

Three teenagers were arrested in Okinawa for allegedly beating a 13-year-old schoolmate to death and burying his body in a cemetery. Now police in Nagasaki are investigating whether the 12-year-old in their custody was involved in molesting four other young children. Police said witnesses had seen a schoolboy with some of the other victims, raising public questions as to whether authorities had taken the previous incidents seriously enough. But others say the spotlight ought to be on Japan's treatment of its children.

They ask whether the society's emphasis on conformity and rules leaves room to deal with the emotions of youngsters. "Japanese society has paid little attention to developing social skills," said Kosuke Yamazaki, principal of a high school in suburban Tokyo and a specialist in child psychiatric medicine. "An increasing number of high school children don't even understand when they are committing a crime. The society needs to teach them more what's right and wrong. The ability of the society to nurture children has diminished."

Children in Japan also are vulnerable as potential victims. They typically walk by themselves to school at a young age, and children often ride buses and subways alone. Japan has not been willing to give up its habits of trust and belief in its safety. Even after a knife-wielding man rampaged through an elementary school in Osaka two years ago, stabbing eight children to death, Japan has been slow to give up freedoms in the name of security, preferring to see those crimes involving children as unique occurrences.

Many of the Japanese media accounts puzzled over the fact that the accused 12-year-old seemed so unlikely a suspect for such a violent act. They carried descriptions of him as a good student, with good grades, who never missed a day of school. "Everybody wants a simple explanation they can understand." (Struck and Sakamaki 2000)

NORWAY

On 15th October 1994, Silje Raedergard was playing with friends on a local football field. She had played with the two boys many times, but this time the game turned rough. Whilst playing snow castles, the two boys became aggressive. They stripped Raedergard, stoned her and when she fell unconscious they panicked and ran, leaving her to die in the snow.

The news of Raedergard's death shocked the small town. With a population of 135,000, the city of Trondheim had only experienced two murders in the six years prior to her death. However instead of expressing anger and revenge, the local community felt grief and a level of responsibility. . . .

In Norway the boys were treated as victims, not killers. The legal age for prosecution stands at 15 and so the children were free to return to kindergarten within a week of the incident occurring.

The local community felt dismayed that such a thing could happen in their city and felt little anger when the two boys were given counseling for the following four years. Trond Andreassen was the head psychologist at the child prosecution agency in Trondheim; he recalls the meetings that he held with the parents of the local kindergarten: "We explained that these boys would start there and what we would do to keep everybody safe. The parents of the other children accepted this situation and a lot of parents thought that these children needed to be in the kindergarten and needed to be taken care of." (BBC World Service 2009)

RUSSIA

Three children aged 10 to 12 have admitted a violent rampage of cruelty in which they beat to death a 10-month old kangaroo and seagulls.

Police in the southern Russian city of Rostov-on-Don say three children confessed to killing the kangaroo and several seagulls over the weekend.

Rostov police spokesman Alexei Polyansky said that the two boys and a girl admitted the killings.

He did not say how the animals were killed, but Russian news reports said they were beaten.

Because the children are minors, their parents could be required to pay fines equivalent to the estimated value of the dead animals—115,000 rubles ($6385).

The zoo's deputy director, Nina Yevtushenko, said its other seven kangaroos are in a state of shock: "In contrast to people, they feel the pain of their relatives." (Three Children Kill Animals 2008)

MIDDLE EAST

"Do you know who I will kill with this gun?" a little boy says into the video camera, waving his toy pistol.

"Who will you kill with this gun?" the cameraman asks.

"The infidels."

The scene appears in a new video by the al-Qaeda-linked Al-Shabab that shows the Somali militant group indoctrinating children, some of whom appear to be toddlers.

Among those seen in the 28-minute video urging the children to fight and become "martyrs" is a former Toronto resident, Omar Hammami, alias Abu Mansour the American.

The video, distributed on the Internet by Al-Shabab's propaganda arm, shows a "children's fair" hosted by Al-Shabab leaders. The boys and girls, identified as the children of "martyrs," are given balloons and snacks and rewarded with toy guns for correctly identifying the late leader of al-Qaeda in Iraq, Abu Musab Al Zarqawi, from a picture. . . .

Instead of playing with toys, these boys are taught to dream about killing infidels. And they kill them afterwards: indoctrination from this age is so powerful. (tea-and-politics.blogspot.com/2010/04/somalia-al-shabab-training-children-to.html)

ISRAEL AND SPAIN

Israel formally protested to Spain's ambassador in Tel Aviv against what appeared to be an orchestrated campaign whereby school children are sending dozens of anti-Israel and anti-Semitic postcards to Israel's ambassador in Madrid.

Naor Gilon, the Foreign Ministry's deputy director-general for western Europe, phoned Spanish ambassador Alvaro Iranzo to protest the postcards, which carried messages such as "why do you kill children?", "Jews kill for money," and "Leave the country for the Palestinians."

Gilon told Iranzo that it was necessary to ensure that Spanish school children were not being "brainwashed," and Iranzo—according to Israeli officials—replied that this was obviously a private initiative and not something condoned by Spain's education ministry.

A spokesman at the Spanish Embassy contacted said it seemed someone was falsifying the true source of the hate mail. He said that the embassy would pass Israel's protest on to Madrid, and that he imagined an investigation would be launched to determine the true source of the postcards. (Keinon 2010)

WORLDWIDE

Flogging, stoning and amputation still used to punish children in detention. Thirty six countries sentence children in conflict with the law to violence such as flogging, stoning and amputation. A further 43 countries still allow corporal punishment to be used against children in detention. . . .

Save the Children is calling for a global ban on all violence committed against children, including those in detention. The need is urgent: 97 per cent of the world's children do not have the same legal protection against violence as adults.

A new Save the Children report, No Place for a Child, highlights the damaging effects of putting children in prison. Latest figures show one million children are in detention, yet few have committed serious or violent crimes. As well as exposing them to abuse, life in detention can leave children feeling isolated, excluded and helpless.

Here are some startling statistics:

- 90% of children in conflict with the law are petty offenders.
- Four out of five children who commit an offence only commit one in their lifetime.
- In the UK, the number of children in detention has more than doubled in the last thirteen years.
- In Kenya, 80–85% of children in police custody or correctional facilities were found to be children in need of care and protection and who had committed no offence.
- In Uganda, 70% of surveyed children in conflict with the law said their main reason for stealing was to get food and meet basic needs.

Leo, 14, Mozambique—"Life in prison is very difficult. We eat badly, we're beaten with a belt, and the cell bosses force us to sleep with them. When we refuse, they beat us. I didn't steal, I didn't kill anybody. I am afraid of dying here."

Jasmine Whitbread, CEO of Save the Children UK "It is shocking that governments are still doing nothing to protect children in conflict with the law. Putting children in detention—often for something as little as stealing bread to survive—and exposing them to such terrible acts of violence, is a massive violation of their rights. It makes them more vulnerable, more alienated and more marginalized."

Save the Children's Day of Action is uniting children across the world to demand world leaders put a stop to violence against children. Events are taking place in countries across six continents in the world's biggest child-led protest against violence.

Save the Children is calling for all governments to

- ban all forms of violence against children wherever they occur
- create an effective national child protection system
- mobilize men and boys in the battle to end violence against children and gender discrimination
- support the appointment of a special representative at the UN to drive forward the global project to end violence against children
- prevent children from coming into conflict with the law, and protect them if they do with child-friendly justice systems.

(Save the Children 2008)

• • •

Violence has no borders or boundaries. It exists where man, woman and child are. It is part of our natures and part of our heritage. Language, cultural differences, cultural rules or expectations do not protect any society from being victimized by youth violence. It is surprising that it does not occur more often given that we have over 6 billion people on earth.

Youth violence is an epidemic that currently runs silently in the underbelly of many societies. In some societies youth violence is buried deep within the system and made to disappear with very little fanfare or social media attention. In others it is in the forefront of the daily news. The responsibility of all nations is on protecting their citizens but overall on producing a next generation that does resort to violence to solve their problems. There will always be youth with pathological problems; the key will be whether that society's structure and expectations are enough to prevent the violence from escalating. There will be occasional incidents in some countries that can lead to discussion and change. It will depend on whether we are paying attention to what is being said and presented to us. Only we, the adults, can impact a youth's life no matter where we are or where we come from.

Epilogue

Youths involved in the ugliness of society become its victims. There are so many shattered lives that began with hope and ended up dead in a dumpster or in a prison cell. What is it about American society that creates this cesspool of hell for juveniles? Why are there so many victims?

Youths who make good choices seemed to be able to navigate the perils of adolescence while so many others cannot. What kinds of characteristics do the successful ones possess? Is it good parenting, effective role models, resiliency, problem solving skills, innate intelligence, positive school experiences or just good genetics?

The only way to understand is to identify the patterns of behavior that seem to be common to certain types of kids or experiences. Chances are very good that if a youth lives in a community with excessive violence and poverty they become poor and violent. If the youth has any aspirations of a better life it often involves drugs and crime to get the fast money they believe will get them out or to escape temporarily.

There is a vast abundance of evidence that shows that if youth become involved in crime they will end up on the streets or in a juvenile detention center or worse, an adult prison. The important factor is to identify an alternative path in the early years. Schools and communities need to invest time and resources to provide these youth with possibilities that will enable them to make better choices.

The school system needs to become more responsive to the needs of the students it is teaching. This educational system needs to get out of the 19th and 20th century and move to teaching the kids of the 21st century. These youths are growing up in a technological age with many new challenges. How effective is the school system at meeting those needs? In my opinion we need to change the way we do business, there are too many lost youths out there roaming the streets of America.

Youth become adults. Youths that are well trained as children with positive experiences in relationships, education, work, and community become functional and productive members of their community as adults. Throw away kids become burdens and dysfunctional adults. They cost the citizens of that community billions of dollars every year to support, manage or detain. The average American is unaware of the costs of keeping a juvenile in detention. Early intervention and support can prevent the downfall into crime or a shortened lifespan because of drug, sexual, or risky behaviors.

Every youth that I interviewed for this book mentioned that they did not want to be on the streets. They wish they could have had a normal life. They hate what their families have done to them. They hate the awful schools they went to, they have no pleasant memories of childhood, because childhood often was full of abuse, dysfunction, and destruction.

Many indicated that they could not fathom a life like they see on television families. Their reality was fueled by drugs, alcohol, early sexual activity, violence, and a constant need to be on alert so that they could survive another day. Their stories reminded me of a small animal in a big forest with many predators around just waiting for them to relax for a second so that they could be captured or killed.

Childhood and adolescence are no longer a blissful time of joy and peace for many American children. It seems from an early onset children are navigating a treacherous route of despair and survival. There are many children and youth who do survive these stages of life but are often scarred in some way. The amount of adults in therapy is extremely high. It seems like no one escapes untouched.

One often wants to blame the parents for all the dysfunctional behaviors of their children. This would be extremely oversimplifying the reasons why children turn to the streets or turn bad. The reasons youths become pathological is based on mental health issues, the formation of cognitive distortions, traumatic experiences, and the lack of development of certain milestones at the right stage of life.

It is very easy to believe that a child is born evil or bad but that would be a coward's way out. The whole argument of nature versus nurture is a powerful argument. The influence of each one of these on the development of a youth at risk can almost be individualized based on the specific youth at risk. We have youths who run away to the streets from very good families and communities. We have youths who seem on the outside equipped with all the necessary skills for a normal life yet they escape to the streets or get caught up in the net of juvenile crime.

There are children who rise up in horrific communities and family situations to become leaders or heroes. Youths who are given the right kinds of opportunities seem to flourish. Being successful seems to depend on whether there is a network of individuals who support and believe in the youth. Encouragement and praise seem to be at the foundation of success.

Being at risk is a statement we hear often within education and politics. We see campaigns to regain the streets, bring youth back to schools, help the poor and homeless, programs to rescue youths, and planned parenthood programs to educate about sex and health and yet so many youths become victims. Why are we so unsuccessful?

The answer is clear in my viewpoint. We have lost the ability to be humanistic, to care for one another in a way that values diversity and differences. We have become judgmental and critical of anything or anyone that is different. We have become so competitive that we will do anything to win. Winning in most cases means that someone else loses and becomes disenfranchised, depressed or devalued. We have lost the ability to be respectful and kind. We are have evolved from the caveman days but only barely when it comes to human interactions and everyday life.

We all seek a certain quality of life to be happy, yet this quality is defined by measures that are not always based in love, trust or positive relationships. It is more often based in power, control and money. The strong survive to dominate another day, the middle men manage to etch out a meager livelihood and be dominated, and the weak become slaves or die. They do not survive another day.

Respect for a human life has various levels of value. In some place the color of your skin or the slant of your eyes dictate whether you will be successful or not. All children are born in this world all equal at birth yet minutes later the perilous journey begins for so many. For some the journey is short and they die because of adverse environmental conditions; others survive to early childhood only to be ravaged by disease or poverty and others survive to adolescence where a whole series of dangerous pits await them. These black holes called sex, alcohol, drugs, violence, and abuse are so prominent that the youth has no chance of making it through. They were born to become a statistic.

Would it not be wonderful if we had a magic wand and could enter every household and grant the necessary skills, intelligence and resources to every parent so that they could raise a normal and functional child? There would no longer be a need for prisons, police, and adults who spend their lives taking care of at-risk kids. We would be in a wonderful place, a place unfortunately that does not exist in America at this time.

It is our mandate as caring and responsible citizens to begin the journey of changing the world we live in. Each of us can make a difference. We have to make a difference with the children and youths we encounter every day. We cannot be callous in our dealings with these kids. We need to care, love, and be available.

Everyday touch a life; it could be what makes a world of difference to a kid in trouble. Look to the sky and see the wonders of the universe and know that a new day will come with new experiences.

References

Adam Walsh Child Protection and Safety Act, retrieved March 3, 2010 from www
.en.wikipedia.org.

AFCARS Report. 2010. U.S. Department of Health and Human Services, Administration for Children and Families, Administration on Children, Youth and Families, Children's Bureau, www.acf.hhs.gov/programs/cb.

American Bar Association Criminal Justice Improvements: Juvenile Justice and Delinquency Prevention Act. Retrieved September 27, 2010, from www.abanet.org/poladv/priorities/juvjustice/.

American Psychiatric Association. 2000. Antisocial Personality Disorder. In *Diagnostic and Statistical Manual of Mental Disorders DSM-IV-TR*. 4th ed. Arlington, VA: www.psychiatryonline.com.

———. 2008. Antisocial Personality Disorder. In R. E. Hales, S.C. Yudofsky, and G. Gabbard, eds. *The American Psychiatric Publishing Textbook of Psychiatry*. 5th ed. Arlington, VA: www.psychiatryonline.com.

Annie E. Casey Foundation. Detention Reform: A Cost-Saving Approach. Available at www.aecf.org/upload/PublicationFiles/jdai_facts1.pdf.

———. Juvenile Detention Initiative Core Standards. Retrieved October 3, 2010, from www.aecf.org/MajorInitiatives/JuvenileDetentionAlternativesInitiative/Core Strategies.aspx.

An Overview of Sex Offenders Management. Retrieved July 2, 2010, www.csom.org/pubs/csom_bro.pdf.

Arya, N., and A. Rolnick. 2008. A Tangled Web of Justice: American Indian and Alaska Native Youth in Federal, State, and Tribal Justice Systems. Washington, DC: Campaign for Youth Justice.

Arya, N., and I. Augarten. 2008. Critical Condition: African-American Youth in the Justice System. Washington, DC: Campaign for Youth Justice.

Arya, N., et al. 2009. America's Invisible Children: Latino Youth and the Failure of Justice. Washington, DC: Campaign for Youth Justice.

Association for the Treatment of Sexual Abusers (ATSA). 2000. Retrieved August 4, 2010, from www.atsa.com/ppjuvenile.html.

Attitudes of US Voters Toward Crime and the US Justice System. 2007. Oakland, CA: National Council on Crime and Delinquency.

Author's Analysis of OJJDP's Census of Juveniles in Residential Placement 1997, 1999, 2001, 2003, and 2006 [machine-readable data files].

Bagley, C., and K. King. 1990. Child Sexual Abuse: The Search for Healing. Tavistock Routledge Press: London.

BBC News Youth and Crimes Report. 2007. Retrieved November 21, 2010, from news.bbc.co.uk/2/hi/6974587.stm.

BBC World Service. 2009. When Children Kill Children. November 9. Available from www.bbc.co.uk/worldservice/people/highlights/001109_child.shtml.

Beck, A., P. Harrison, and P. Guerino. 2010. Sexual Victimization in Juvenile Facilities Reported by Youth, 2008–2009.Washington, DC: U.S. Department of Justice, Office of Justice Programs, Bureau of Justice Statistics.

Beck, A. J., P. M. Harrison, and D. B. Adams. 2007. Sexual Violence Reported by Correctional Authorities, 2006. Washington, DC: U.S. Department of Justice, Office of Justice Programs, Bureau of Justice Statistics.

Blueprint for Juvenile Justice Reform. 2006. Retrieved July 2010 from www.ytfg.org/documents/Platform_Juvenile_Justice.pdf.

Bookman, S. 2010. 5 SI Teens Arrested on Hate Crime Charges. October 11. Retrieved December 12, 2010, from .abclocal.go.com/wabc/story?section=news/local&id=7718678.

Booth, C. 2002. Institute for Family Development. Available from www.strengthening families.org/html/programs_1999/23_HOMEBUILDERS.html.

Boston Ten Point Coalition. Retrieved December 5, 2010, from www.bostontenpoint .org.

Bynum, J. E., and W. E. Thompson. 1996. Juvenile Delinquency: A Sociological Approach. 3d ed. Needham Heights, MA: Allyn and Bacon.

California Court Self Help Center: Introduction to Juvenile Court. Retrieved October 3, 2010, from www.courtinfo.ca.gov/selfhelp/family/juv/intro.htm.

Campaign For Youth Justice Newsletter 2007: Campaign for Youth Justice Because the Consequences aren't Minor. Retrieved September 21, 2010 from www .campaignforyouthjustice.org/documents/November2007Newslettersent.pdf

Center for Children's Law and Policy: Building Blocks for Youth. Juvenile Detention Alternatives. Retrieved from www.cclp.org/JDAI.php.

Center for Sex Offender Management (CSOM). 2007. Enhancing the Management of Adult and Juvenile Sex Offenders: A Handbook for Policymakers and Practitioners. Retrieved August 4, 2010, from www.csom.org/pubs/CSOM_handbook.pdf.

Center on Juvenile and Criminal Justice. Resources retrieved November 11, 2010 from www.cjcj.org/juvenile/justice/juvenile/justice/overview.

Centers for Disease Control and Prevention. 2007. Web-based Injury Statistics Query and Reporting System (WISQARS) [Online]. National Center for Injury Prevention and Control, Centers for Disease Control and Prevention (producer) [2010 June 14]. Available at www.cdc.gov/injury.

Chang, L. 2001. Bitter Teenage Crime. *Shanghai Star.* August 16.

Children Defense Freedom Schools. 2010. Retrieved Dec 5, 2010 from www .freedomschools.org.

Children's Bureau AFCARS Report. 2008. Cited at www.adoptionlearningpartners. org/foster_to_forever.cfm.

Children's Congress on Sexual Exploitation. Stockholm 1996 and Yokohama 2001. Retrieved October 2, 2010 from www.csecworldcongress.org.

Children's Mental Health Disorder Fact Sheet for the Classroom. Reactive Attachment Disorder *(RAD).* Retrieved July 18, 2010, from www.ksde.org/KS_SAFE_ SCHOOLS_RESOURCE_CENTER/RAD.pdf.

Cohen, M. A., and A. R. Piquero. 2007). New Evidence on the Monetary Value of Saving a High Risk Youth. Vanderbilt Law and Economics Research Paper No. 08–07, available at ssrn.com/abstract=1077214.

Cohen, Tamara. 2010. Girls "Kicked Gay Man to Death in Attack like Scene from *A Clockwork Orange." Daily Mail.* April 20. Accessed July 1, 2011 at www .dailymail.co.uk/news/article-1267283/Girls-kicked-gay-man-Ian-Baynham -death-Clockwork-Orange-style-attack.html.

Cornell University Law School. Retrieved October 24, 2010, from www.law.cornell. edu/supct/.

Corner School Development Program. Retrieved December 5, 2010, from www .schooldevelopmentprogram.org.

Coslett, P. 2006. Murder of James Bulger. *The Times.* April 12. Available from www.bbc.co.uk/liverpool/content/articles/2006/12/04/local_history_bulger_ feature.shtml.

Cutting and Self-harm. Retrieved July 3, 2010 from helpguide.org/mental/self-injury .htm.

Cutting Statistics and Self-Injury Treatment. Retrieved July 3, 2010, from www .teenhelp.com/teen-health/cutting-stats-treatment.html.

Daily Telegraph. 2010. Thugs Assault Students in School Fight. February 18. Available from www.dailytelegraph.com.au/news/thugs-involved-in-school-fight/ story-e6freuy9-1225831555846.

Dead Silence. The Kobe School Killer. Available from deadsilence.wordpress .com/2006/07/15/the-kobe-school-killer/.

Dowsley, A. 2007. Wild Teen Crime Wave Includes Stabbing Charge. *Herald Sun.* November 13.

Duggan, C. 2009. A Treatment Guideline for People with Antisocial Personality Disorder: Overcoming Attitudinal Barriers and Evidential Limitations. *Criminal Behaviour & Mental Health* 19(4): 219–23.

Edelman, Marian Wright. 2006. Losing The Children Early and Often. Retrieved July 6, 2010 from cdf.childrensdefense.org/site/DocServer/Losing_the_Children_ Early_and_Often-_Crisis_Mag.pdf?docID=4103.

Effective Legal Management of Juvenile Sex Offenders. Retrieved June 2, 2010 from www.asta.com/ppjuvenile.html.

Family Watch Dog FAQ Definition of Sex Offenders. Retrieved August 20, 2010 fromwww.familywatchdog.us/laws/COlaws.asp.

Federal Bureau of Investigation. 2008. Crime in the United States. Washington, D.C. Retrieved October 26, 2009, from www.fbi.gov/ucr/cius2008/data/table_28.html.

Frontline. 2001. Manny and Shawn. Stories of Juvenile Justice. (1995–2011). Retrieved December 12, 2010, from www.pbs.org/wgbh/pages/frontline/shows/juvenile/four/manny.html.

Grisso, Thomas. 2008. Adolescent Offenders with Mental Health Disorders. *Future of Children* 18 (2). Retrieved July 2010 at www.futureofchildren.org.

Gupta, Prakriiti. 2007, The Deadly Trade of Child Organ Trafficking. Retrieved from www.aawsat.com/english/news.asp?section=3&id=7723.

Harlem Children's Zone: Special Project. Retrieved October 23, 2010 from www.hcz.org.

Harrison, P. M., and D. B. Adams. 2007. Sexual Violence Reported by Correctional Authorities, 2005. Washington, DC: U.S. Department of Justice, Office of Justice Programs, Bureau of Justice Statistics.

Harvard Mental Health Letter. 2000. Antisocial Personality--Part I., 17(6): 1. Retrieved from EBSCO*host*.

Hawkins, D., and R. Catalano. 2002. Preparing for the Drug Free Years. Available from www.strengtheningfamilies.org/html/programs_1999/05_PDFY.html.

Hemphill, C. 2009. Where the Sick Get Sicker. *Child Welfare Watch* 18 (Fall): 5–9. Available from www.newschool.edu/milano/nycaffairs/CWW_18_third_article.aspx.

Herrenkohl, T. I., et al. 2001. School and Community Risk Factors and Interventions. In *Child Delinquents: Development, Intervention, and Service Needs,* ed. R. Loeber and D. P. Farrington. Thousand Oaks, CA: Sage, 211–46.

Hesse, M. 2010. What Should Be Done with Antisocial Personality Disorder in the New Edition of the Diagnostic and Statistical Manual of Mental Disorders (DSM-V)? *BMC Medicine*, 866–69.

History of American Juvenile Justice System. Lawyershop.com. Retrieved Oct 2, 2010, from www.lawyershop.com/practice-areas/criminal-law/juvenile-law/history/.

Holman, B., and J. Ziedenberg. 2006. The Dangers of Detention: The Impact of Incarcerating Youth in Detention and Other Secure Facilities. Washington, DC. Justice Policy Institute.

Human Rights Watch. 2009. State Distribution of Estimated 2,574 Juvenile Offenders Serving Life without Parole. New York, NY. Retrieved October 26, 2009, from www.hrw.org/en/news/2009/10/02/state-distribution-juvenile-offenders-serving-juvenile-life-without-parole.

Investigative Discovery: Crime Countdown 2008. Retrieved August 5, 2010 from investigation.discovery.com/investigation/crime-countdowns/crime-stories/crime-stories-07.html.

The Independent. 2010. The End of Innocence: Inside Britain's Child Prisons. January 21. Available from www.independent.co.uk/news/uk/crime/the-end-of-innocence-inside-britains-child-prisons-1874053.html.

Jailing Juveniles. 2007. Washington, DC: Campaign for Youth Justice.

Juvenile Detention Alternatives Initiative. Detention Reform: An Effective Public Safety Strategy. Retrieved October 9, 2008, from www.jdaihelpdesk.org/Docs/Documents/z%20044-07_JDAI_factsheet2_r13bl.pdf

Juvenile Detention Alternatives Initiative. 2007. Detention Reform Brief 1: Detention Reform: A Cost-Saving Approach. Annie E. Casey Foundation. Available from www.aecf.org/upload/PublicationFiles/jdai_facts1.pdf.

Juvenile Justice Process. 2008. Lawyershop.com. Retrieved October 3, 2010, from www.lawyershop.com/practice-areas/criminal-law/juvenile-law/history/.

Juvenile Justice Reform. Retrieved September 27, 2010, from www.ytfg.org/documents/Platform_Juvenile_Justice.pdf.

Juvenile Offenders and Victims National Report. 2006. US Department of Justice, Office of Justice Programs, Office of Juvenile Justice Programs, Office of Juvenile Justice and Delinquency Prevention.

Keinon, H. 2010. Israel Protests Hate-Filled Postcards from Spanish Kids. *Jerusalem Post*. March 1. Retrieved July 2, 2011, from www.jpost.com/Israel/Article.aspx?id=169885.

Koenigsburg, J. 2008–2010. Juvenile Sex Offenders. Retrieved August 2, 2010, from www.horses-helping-troubled-teens.com/juvenile-sex-offenders.html.

LaBelle, D. 2005. Testimony Before the National Prison Rape Elimination Commission. At Risk: Sexual Abuse and Vulnerable Groups Behind Bars. August 19. 33.

La Voz de Aztlan. 2010. Haitian Prime Minister Confirms Trafficking in Human Organs. January 29. Retrieved January 2010, from www.atlzan.net.

Leone, P., M. Quinn, and D. Osher. 2002. Collaboration in the Juvenile Justice System and Youth Serving Agencies: Improving Prevention, Providing More Efficient Services, and Reducing Recidivism for Youth with Disabilities. Washington, DC: American Institutes for Research. Retrieved February 1, 2010, from cecp.air.org/juvenilejustice/docs/Collaboration%20in%20the%20Juvenile%20Justice%20System.pdf.

Levinson, H. 2001. Japanese Juvenile Justice. *BBC World Service*. February 24. Retrieved July 2, 2011, from www.bbc.co.uk/worldservice/people/highlights/010223_japan.shtml.

Lipsey, M. W., and J. H. Derzon. 1998. Predictors of Violent and Serious Delinquency in Adolescence and Early Adulthood: A Synthesis of Longitudinal Research. In *Serious and Violent Juvenile Offenders: Risk Factors and Successful Interventions*, ed. R. Loeber and D. P. Farrington. Thousand Oaks, CA: Sage, 86–105.

Livsey, S., M. Sickmund, and A. Sladky. 2009. Juvenile Residential Facility Census, 2004: Selected Findings. Washington, DC: U.S. Department of Justice, Office of Justice Programs, Office of Juvenile Justice and Delinquency Prevention.

Lundman, R. J. 1993. *Prevention and Control of Delinquency*. 2d ed. New York: Oxford University Press.

McDougal, B. 2010. Thugs Involved in School Fight. The Daily Telegraph. February. Available from www.dailytelegraph.com.au/news/thugs-involved-in-school-fight/story-e6freuy9-1225831555846.

Mckay, M. J. 2003. Life in Prison: Felony Murder. January 29. Available from www.cbsnews.com/stories/2003/01/29/60II/main538407.shtml.

McMaster, N. 2009. 3 Teens Set Another on Fire, Police Say. October 13. Available from www.newser.com/story/71612/3-teens-set-another-on-fire-police-say.html.

Mercy, J., et al. 2002. Youth Violence. In World Report on Violence and Health, ed. E. Krug, et al. Geneva: World Health Organization: 25–56.

Miller, W., et al. 1995. Motivational Enhancement Therapy Manual: A Clinical Resource Guide for Therapist Treating Individuals with Alcohol Abuse and Dependence. The National Institute on Alcohol Abuse and Alcoholism Project MATCH Monograph Series, vol. 2. Washington, D.C.: U.S. Department of Health and Human Services.

Moore, S. 2009. Prisons Becoming Asylums for Mentally Ill Youth. *New York Times.* August 10.

Morrison, B. 2002. Bullying and Victimisation in Schools: A Restorative Justice Approach. *Trends & Issues in Crime and Criminal Justice* 219. Canberra, Australia: Australian Institute of Criminology. Retrieved October 3, 2010 from www.aic.gov. au/publications/tandi/ti219.pdf.

Mountain Homes Youth Ranch Program. www.mhyr.com/program/our-program-1 .html.

National Association of Cognitive Behavioral Therapists. 2009. Cognitive Behavioral Therapy. Retrieved on August 4, 2010, from www.nacbt.org/whatiscbt.htm.

National Crime Prevention Council. Programs to Reduce Juvenile Violence. Retrieved October, 3, 2010, from www.ncpc.org/topics/school-safety/strategies/ strategy-training-school-personnel-in-crime-prevention.

National Data Archive on Child Abuse and Neglect. 2007. National Child Abuse and Neglect Data Systems, retrieved July 28, 2010 from www.ndacan.cornell.edu/ index.html.

National Institute of Health National Library of Medicine, Cognitive Effects of Metal Toxicity. Retrieved February 5, 2010 from www.nlm.nih.gov.

National Juvenile Detention Center. National Juvenile Corrections Data Resource Guide. Retrieved September 2010 from www.icpsr.umich.edu/NACJD/njcd/.

National Prison Rape Elimination Commission Report 18. 2009. Available from www.ncjrs.gov/pdffiles1/226680.pdf.

Nicola, S. 2008. Analysis: Youth Crime Shocks Germany. January 9. Available from www.upi.com/Top_News/Special/2008/01/09/Analysis-Youth-crime-shocks -Germany/UPI-23501199908648/.

O'Brien, M. J., and W. H. Bera. 1992. Typology of Adolescent Sexual Offenders: Program for Healthy Adolescent Sexual Expression and Phases. Maplewood, Minnesota.

Office of Juvenile Justice and Delinquency Prevention. CeaseFire Chicago. Available from www.ojjdp.gov/mpg/mpgProgramDetails.aspx?ID=835.

Operation Cease Fire. Retrieved December 5, from dakennedy@jjay.cuny.edu.

The Pace Center for Girls. Retrieved December 5, 2010, from www.pacecenter.org.

Puzzanchera, C., Adams, B., Sickmund, M. (2010).Juvenile Court Statistics 2006– 2007.Pittsburgh, PA: National Center for Juvenile Justice.

Quinn, R. 2010. 13 Year Old Boy Spared Life Sentence: Detroit Boy to Stay in Juvenile Detention until He Turns 21. Newser. June 18.

Redding, R. E. 2008. Juvenile Transfer Laws: An Effective Deterrent to Delinquency? Washington, D.C.: U.S. Department of Justice, Office of Justice Programs, Office of Juvenile Justice and Delinquency Prevention.

Resnick, M. D., M. Ireland, and I. Borowsky. 2004. Youth Violence Perpetration: What Protects? What Predicts? Findings from the National Longitudinal Study of Adolescent Health. *Journal of Adolescent Health* 35(424):1–10.

Richardson, K. 2010. Anti-Gay Gang Torture Suspects Arraigned. October 11. Retrieved December 12, 2010, from abclocal.go.com/wabc/story?section=news/local&id=7716206.

Ries, R. 1994. Assessment and Treatment of Patients with Coexisting Mental Illness and Alcohol and Other Drug Abuse. Rockville, MD: U.S. Department of Health and Human Services, Substance Abuse and Mental Health Service Administration, Center for Substance Abuse Treatment.

Robinson, D. A., and O. H. Stephens. 1992. Patterns of Mitigating Factors in Juvenile Death Penalty Cases. *Criminal Law Bulletin* 28(3): 246–75.

Save the Children. 2008. Flogging, Stoning, and Amputation Still Used to Punish Children in Detention. Press release. Retrieved on July 2, 2011, from www.savethe children.net/alliance/media/newsdesk/2006-10-09a.html.

Schechter, H. 2003. *The Serial Killer Files*. New York: Ballantine.

School Boy Killer Gets Life Term. 2004. BBC News. July 27. Retrieved December 12, 2010, from news.bbc.co.uk/2/hi/uk_news/england/lincolnshire/3929015.stm.

School Violence, Weapons, Crimes and Bullying. Retrieved September 12, 2010, from www.nssc1.org/.

Sedlack, A., and K. McPherson. 2010. Conditions of Confinement: Findings from the Survey of Youth in Residential Placement. Washington, DC: U.S. Department of Justice, Office of Justice Programs, Office of Juvenile Justice and Delinquency Prevention.

Sickmund, M. 2010. Juveniles in Residential Placement, 1997–2008. Washington, DC: U.S. Department of Justice, Office of Justice Programs, Office of Juvenile Justice and Delinquency Prevention.

Sickmund, M., T. J. Sladky, W. Kang, and C. Puzzanchera. 2008. Easy Access to the Census of Juveniles in Residential Placement. Available from ojjdp.ncjrs.gov/ojstatbb/ezacjrp/.

Sickmund, M., T. J. Sladky, and W. Kang. 2008. Census of Juveniles in Residential Placement Databook. Available from www.ojjdp.ncjrs.gov/ojstatbb/cjrp/.

Snyder, H. N. 2001. Epidemiology of Official Offending. In *Child Delinquents: Development, Intervention, and Service Needs*, ed. R. Loeber and D. P. Farrington. Thousand Oaks, CA: Sage, 25–46.

Sociopathic Behaviors in Children. Retrieved September 4, 2010 from www.buzzle.com.

Spagat, E. 2010. Teen Gets 40 Years for Killing California Border Agent. April 30. Available from www.policeone.com/juvenile-crime/articles/2055951 -Teen-gets-40-years-for-killing-Calif-border-agent/.

Stenhjem, P. 2005. Youth with Disabilities in the Juvenile Justice System: Prevention and Intervention Strategies. Examining Current Challenges in Secondary Education and Transition 4(1).

Streib, V. L. 2000. The Juvenile Death Penalty Today: Death Sentences and Executions for Juvenile Crimes, January 1, 1973–June 30, 2000. Ada, OH: Ohio Northern University, Claude W. Pettit College of Law.

Struck, D., and S. Sakamaki. 2003. Boy Killer Makes Japan Cry for Medieval Justice. July 13. Available from www.indianexpress.com/oldStory/27563/.

Tea and Politics Blog. tea-and-politics.blogspot.com/2010/04/somalia-al-shabab -training-children-to.html.

Teen Girls Face Charges for Fliers. 2007. May 23. Retrieved December 12, 2010, from www.foxnews.com/sitemap/0,4937,80,00.html.

Teen Murderer Says Jail Is Too Hard, Appeals Sentence. 2006. December 6. Available from www.wftv.com/news/10458584/detail.html.

Three Children Kill Animals. 2008. *The Daily Telegraph*. October 24. Available from www.dailytelegraph.com.au/news/world/three-children-kill-kangaroo -seagulls-in-russia/story-e6frev00-1111117841496.

Trafficking in Children for Sexual Purposes: An Analytical Review. 2001. Theme paper for the 2nd world congress against the Commercial Sexual Exploitation of Children, Yokohama, 19. Available from www.csecworldcongress.org/PDF/ en/Yokohama/Background_reading/Theme_papers/Theme paper Trafficking in Children.pdf.

Twisted Minds. Retrieved August 5, 2010 from www.twistedminds.creativescapism. com/psychological_disorders.

Umbreit, M. 2000. *Family Group Conferencing: Implications for Crime Victims*. St. Paul: University of Minnesota, School of Social Work, Center for Restorative Justice and Peacemaking.

Umbreit, M., and C. Fercello. 1997. Interim Report: Client Evaluation of the Victim/ Offender Conferencing Program in Washington County (MN). St. Paul: University of Minnesota, School of Social Work, Center for Restorative Justice and Peacemaking.

Underwood, L. A., L. Barretti, T. L. Storms, N. Safonte-Strumbolo. 2004. A Review of Clinical Characteristics and Residential Treatments for Adolescent Males with Mental Health Disorders: A Promising Program. *Journal of Trauma, Violence and Abuse* 5(3): 199–242.

Underwood, L. A., W. C. Mullan, and C. L. Walter. 1997. We Built Them and They Came: New Insights for Managing Ohio's Aggressive Juvenile Offenders with Mental Illness. *Corrections Management Quarterly* 1(4): 19–27.

Underwood, L. A., K. Phillips, K. Von Dresner, and P. D. Knight. 2006. Critical Factors in Mental Health Programming for Juveniles in Correction Facilities. *International Journal of Behavioral Consultation and Therapy* 2(1).

UNICEF. Child Trafficking. Retrieved December 26, 2010, from www.unicef.org/ protection/index_exploitation.html.

U.S. Department of Commerce, Bureau of the Census, July 1, 2008. Estimates of the Resident Population by Selected Age Groups for the United States and Puerto Rico.

Vasil, J. 2000. Decision-Making Scenarios. www.pecentral.org.

What is Child Pornography? Retrieved December 26, 2010, from www.missingkids .com/missingkids/servlet/PageServlet?LanguageCountry=en_US&PageId=1504.

Woolard, J. 2005. Juveniles within Adult Correctional Settings: Legal Pathways and Developmental Considerations. *International Journal of Forensic Mental Health* 4(1).

World Net Daily. 2003.. Boy Who Killed Girl: I Did Her a Favor. December 12. Available from www.wnd.com/news/article.asp?article_id=36095.

Yourbloodismyblood blog. Accessed July 2, 2011 at http://yourbloodismyblood .blogspot.com/.

Youth Advocate Programs. 2011. www.yapinc.org/index.php?pID=273.

About the Author

Dr. Marcel Lebrun has been an educator for thirty-two years. During that time he has been a classroom teacher, administrator, school counselor, and special education teacher. He was the director of a stress and anxiety clinic from 1994 to 2002 and a university counselor from 2002 to 2005.

He is presently a professor and chair at Plymouth State University in the Department of Education. He teaches classes in special education, behavior management, and educational methodology at the undergraduate and graduate level. He has taught abroad and traveled extensively throughout the world. Lebrun has published several books on depression, sexual orientation, school shootings, violence and aggression in teenagers and children, and academic strategies.

In the fall of 2011 his eighth book will be released. He has published several articles on behavior issues and mental health concerns in children.

He is presently on the leadership team for the Positive Behavior Intervention and Supports initiative in New Hampshire. He also provides consulting services to several school districts in need of improvement with handling behavior issues and school-wide intervention and supports. Lebrun works mostly with school personnel around student issues in violence, aggression, functional assessment, and mental health concerns. He has presented throughout the United States, Canada, Europe, Africa and Asia. Dr. Lebrun was honored with Distinguished Professor of the Year for 2008. He has presented at Harvard Medical School and Oxford University in England. He recently returned from doing some work in Namibia.

He is an active member of many professional organizations: the International Association of Special Education, the Council for Children with Behavior Disorders, and the Council of Exceptional Children.

Dr. Lebrun is a colorful and energetic professor, writer, and activist for change when it comes to better schools, better children, and a peaceful and kinder society.

CPSIA information can be obtained at www.ICGtesting.com
Printed in the USA
BVOW040409061211

277647BV00002B/5/P